INTO THE ABYSS

THE LAST YEARS OF THE WAFFEN SS 1943–45

A Photographic History

Ian Baxter

HELION & COMPANY

Helion & Company Limited
26 Willow Road
Solihull
West Midlands
B91 1UE
England
Tel. 0121 705 3393
Fax 0121 711 4075
Email: publishing@helion.co.uk
Website: http://www.helion.co.uk

Published by Helion & Company 2006
Designed and typeset by Helion & Company Limited, Solihull, West Midlands
Cover designed by Bookcraft Limited, Stroud, Gloucestershire
Printed by Cromwell Press Ltd, Trowbridge, Wiltshire

Text © Ian Baxter 2006
Photographs © History in the Making Archive
Maps © Helion & Company Ltd.

ISBN 1 874622 59 0

British Library Cataloguing-in-Publication Data.
A catalogue record for this book is available from the British Library.

For details of other military history titles published by Helion & Company Limited contact the above address, or visit our website: http://www.helion.co.uk.

We always welcome receiving book proposals from prospective authors.

Contents

Foreword

Into the Abyss: The Last Years of the Waffen-SS 1943–45 is an in-depth record of the elite Waffen-SS divisions that fought both on the Eastern and Western Fronts during the last two years of the war. Drawing on previously unpublished photographs, many of which have come from the albums of individuals that experienced and took part in the war, the book presents a unique account of one of military history's most infamous wars.

From its new organisation and development in 1943 the book describes the fighting tactics, the uniforms, the battles and the different elements that went into making the Waffen-SS such an elite fighting unit, in spite of being in the death throes of loosing the war. It describes how the Waffen-SS carefully built up their assault forces utilising all available reserves and resources thus making it an effective killing machine. It depicts how this awesome machine grew to be used in defensive battles, and provides much historical information and facts about the weapons and all the components that fought in the final battles on the Eastern and Western Fronts. Throughout the chapters it describes how the Waffen-SS evolved and how they were shifted from one disintegrating part of the front to another in a drastic attempt to stabilise the crumbling war effort.

With over 180 unpublished photographs, illustrations and text, Into the Abyss: The Last Years of the Waffen-SS brings together a captivating glimpse at the full workings of one of the most effective weapons ever used in military history.

Photographic Acknowledgements

It is with the greatest pleasure that I use this opportunity on concluding this book to thank those who helped make this volume possible. My expression of gratitude first goes to my German photographic collector Rolf Halfen. He has been an unfailing source, supplying me with a number of very rare *Waffen-SS* photographs that were obtained from numerous private sources. Throughout the research stage of this book Rolf searched and contacted numerous collectors all over Germany, trying in vain to find late *SS* photographs. Unfortunately, some collectors would not part with their prized *SS* images, which made finding them so much harder. Late photographs like *Wiking, Nord, Hohenstaufen,* and *Frundsberg* together with late armoured vehicles used by the *SS* were difficult, to say the least, to find unpublished. I had numerous researchers trying to locate these elusive photographs, but it was Rolf once again that managed to find them in private photo collections in Germany.

Further afield in Poland I am also extremely grateful to Marcin Kaludow, my Polish photographic specialist, who supplied me with a number of rare photographs that he obtained from private photographic collections in Poland, Russia and the Ukraine. The images he found show a host of interesting photographs showing the *Waffen-SS* during the famous battle at Kursk, fighting for the city of Kharkov, winter and summer battles during 1944, and a unique batch of photos showing *SS* troops and armoured regiments fighting in Poland during the last desperate months of the war.

Finally, I wish to display my kindness and appreciation to my American photographic collector, Richard White, who supplied me with a number of rare unpublished photographs showing the *Waffen-SS* deployed both on the Eastern and Western Fronts.

Introduction

Between 1933 and 1939, the power of the *SS* grew considerably with thousands of men being recruited into the new ideological elite armed formation under the command of Heinrich Himmler. All early recruits were expected to meet very stringent criteria. Every volunteer had to be fit with excellent racial features and produce a certificate of good behaviour from the Police. During their tough training programme new recruits was indoctrinated into an almost fanatical determination to fight for the *Führer*, even if it meant shedding one's own blood on the battlefield. With blind allegiance the recruit was to step out and join one of the newly-created armed *SS* divisions where he would obey every order, even if it meant shooting prisoners and committing atrocities against civilians.

These new recruits of the *SS* eventually put into practice their training and indoctrination and wreaked death and destruction on their foe. During the first half of the war the *Waffen-SS* had consistently performed with unshakable tenacity. On the Eastern Front the classic divisions like the *Leibstandarte Adolf Hitler*, *Das Reich* and *Totenkopf*, won the confidence and gratitude of their beloved *Führer*. By late 1942 the *Waffen-SS* still displayed the ability to retain its fighting spirit, even as the tide of war slowly turned against them. While many *Wehrmacht* units and their commanders withdrew in the face of growing Russian resistance, the *Waffen-SS* stood firm.

It was this endurance, coupled by skill and tenacity by the *SS* in Russia that led to Hitler's decision to expand the *Waffen-SS*. Initially, he had been against expanding, but by late 1942 the events on the Eastern Front had forced him to give up his earlier optimism and face facts that the war would be a long drawn out battle of attrition. By 1 September 1942, the *Waffen-SS* had a field strength of 141,975 men with an additional 45,663 in training and reserve. Exactly a year later that figure had almost doubled to 280,000 in the field units and 70,000 in training and reserve.

During this period of expansion the *Waffen-SS* for the first time had to resort to the large-scale conscription of foreign recruits. Thousands of youths who met *SS* standards were drafted from the work camps of the *Reich* Labour Service. Nordic volunteers and *Volksdeutsche* – people of Germanic descent from countries in Eastern Europe helped dilute the so-called pure Nordic stock with foreign blood. Over the next two years this expansion saw the final *Waffen-SS* order of battle of thirty-eight divisions, though the later divisions never approached the proper level of manpower. Foreign soldiers prominently manned many of these divisions. Only about twelve of the divisions were a true elite; most were formed late in the war and were divisions in name only, often being poorly equipped.

Between February and July 1943 the *Waffen-SS* underwent a large expansion. The 9.*SS.Panzergrenadier-Division Hohenstaufen* and the 10.*SS.Panzergrenadier-Division Frundsberg* were being formed. In March, the 11.*SS.Freiwilligen*-Panzergrenadier-Division *Nordland* was created by merging the four Germanic legions, units from the 5.*SS.Division Wiking*, and a large group of new West European recruits. In the spring, the 12.*SS.Panzergrenadier*-Division *Hitlerjugend*, were officially activated. During this period, three eastern *SS* divisions were established.

Whilst the best efforts were made to expand the *Waffen-SS*, during the first half of 1943, the elite combat formations saw extensive action and were continuously being shuttled from one danger spot to another, with only a brief rest for refitting. These *SS* Panzer and Panzergrenadier divisions had become known as the fire brigade of the *Third Reich*. Wherever they were committed to battle, they attacked. Sometimes the outcome was successful, but there were many times when they failed. But whatever the outcome of the individual action, the end mostly resulted in delaying the enemy advance. This had become the value of the *Waffen-SS* in the last two years of the war.

In these last years, the deciding factors in ground warfare were the Panzer, self-propelled artillery, and mechanised infantry. They had become such an important bearing to the successful continuation of the war that seven of the thirty Panzer divisions and six Panzergrenadier divisions in the *Wehrmacht* became elite *Waffen-SS* formations. These seven divisions became Hitler's emergency fire brigade, with the occasional assistance from a number of less elite *SS*-Panzergrenadier divisions.

Hitler looked upon these divisions to blunt the Soviet offensive that had already gained the initiative following the destruction of the 6.*Armee* at Stalingrad. As far as he was concerned, the SS had stood firm in the face of adversity – unlike the *Wehrmacht*. In March 1943, Hitler was proved correct when three of his elite divisions *Leibstandarte Adolf Hitler*, *Das Reich*, and *Totenkopf* of the newly formed *SS-Panzer-Korps* recaptured the city of Kharkov.

After stemming the Soviets at Kharkov, the *SS-Panzer-Korps* were prepared to spearhead the German summer offensive on the central sector of the Eastern Front, in the area of Orel and Kursk. This would be the last major offensive operation undertaken by the Germans in the East. What would follow in its wake would be almost two years of bitter, bloody defensive battles with the *Waffen-SS* being rushed to one disintegrating sector of the front to another, plugging the gaps and fighting to the death in order to slow-down the inevitable advance of the Red Army.

PART I

Combat Deployment in the East Summer-Winter 1943

1. Operation *Zitadelle*

In July 1943, German combat formations launched what proved to be their last great offensive on the Eastern Front – against the Kursk salient. Despite massive losses sustained by their forces at Stalingrad, which led to the subsequent destruction of 6.*Armee*, Hitler was determined as ever not to give up the fight in Russia. It was at Kursk that the *Führer* was confronted with a very tempting strategic opportunity that he was convinced could yield him victory.

Within the huge salient, measuring some 120 miles wide and 75 miles deep, he tried to persuade his commanders that his force could attack from north and south of the salient in a huge pincer movement and encircle the Red Army. In Hitler's view, the offensive would be the greatest armoured battle ever won on the Eastern Front and would include the bulk of his mighty *Panzerwaffe*, among them his elite *Waffen-SS* divisions.

The offensive, code-named operation *Zitadelle*, would smash Red Army formations and leave the road to Moscow open. For this daring offensive, the German force were distributed between the Northern and Southern groups, consisting of a total of twenty-two divisions, six of which were Panzer and five Panzergrenadier. The main attack fell to the 9.*Armee* in the north. There were some 335,000 soldiers, 590 tanks and 424 assault guns. In the south, the Germans fielded a much stronger force and concentrated 349,907 troops, 1,269 tanks and 245 assault guns. Although it was a formidable assembly of firepower with 102 Tiger tanks, it was, in fact, facing an even greater enemy, coupled with almost impregnable defensive belts.

In the Kursk salient the Russians had constructed more than six of these major defensive belts, each of which were subdivided into two or even three layers of well-defended strongholds. The first two belts were occupied by troops, while units that were held in reserve occupied the third and fourth belts. The last two belts were virtually empty of soldiers and used mainly to pour reserves in if the need arose. Each belt was a maze of intricate blockhouses and trenches. In some areas of the belt the Russians had emplaced more than 70,000 anti-tank and 64,000 anti-personnel mines.

In front of the Soviet defensive fortress stood the cream of all the German combat formations at Kursk, the premier divisions of the *Waffen-SS*. In *Heeresgruppe Süd* these elite soldiers were deployed for action, ready at a moment's notice to fight their way through the formidable lines of barbed wire entanglements, mine fields and anti-tank guns. Here, the II.*SS.Panzer-Korps*, commanded by *SS-Obergruppenführer* Paul Hausser, formed part of the 4.*Panzer-Armee*. The *Korps* comprised of the three premiere *Waffen-SS* divisions, 1.*SS. Leibstandarte Adolf Hitler* Division, the 2.*SS. Das Reich* Division and the 3.*SS.Totenkopf* Division. The three divisions had a line strength of 390 of the latest tanks and 104 assault guns between them, including 42 of the Army Group's Tigers. At their starting positions, the three *SS* divisions covered a sector that was 12 miles wide. The *Totenkopf* occupied the left flank of the advance, the *Leibstandarte* was in the centre and *Das Reich* held the right.

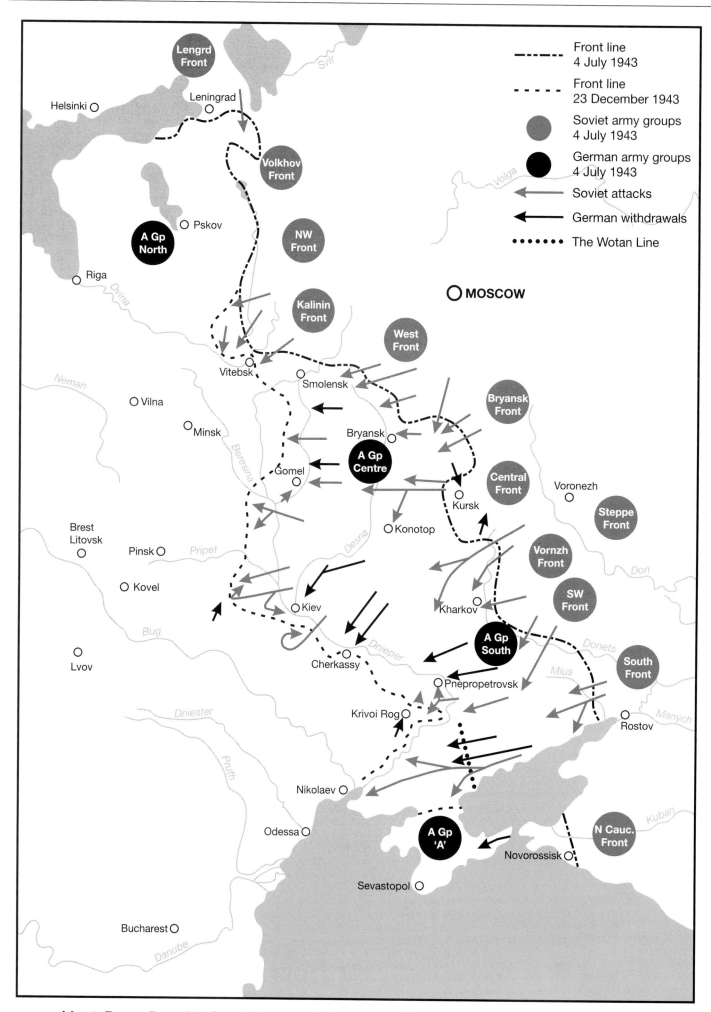

Map 1: Eastern Front, Kursk and subsequent Soviet counter-offensives and offensives, July-December 1943

Waffen-SS Kursk Order of Battle[1]
II.SS.Panzer-Korps – SS. Obergruppenführer Paul Hausser

1.SS. Panzergrenadier-Division *Leibstandarte Adolf Hitler*

SS. *Brigadeführer* Wisch
1.*SS.* Panzer-Regiment, 1.*SS.* Panzer Grenadier-Regiment, 2.*SS.* Panzergrenadier-Regiment, 1.*SS.*Panzer-Artillerie-Regiment, I.*SS.*Panzer-Reconnaissance-Bataillon, I. *SS.*Panzer-Engineer-Bataillon, I.*SS.*Flak-Bataillon
Strength: 106 tanks and 35 assault guns

2.SS.Panzergrenadier-Division *Das Reich*

SS.*Grupppenführer* Kruger
1.*SS.*Panzer-Regiment, 3.*SS.*Panzergrenadier-Regiment *Deutschland,* 4.*SS.*Panzergrenadier-Regiment *Der Führer,* 2.*SS.*Panzer-Artillerie-Regiment, 2.*SS.*Panzer-Reconnaissance-Bataillon, 2.*SS.*Flak-Bataillon, 2.*SS.*Panzer-Engineer-Bataillon, 2.*SS.*Flak-Bataillon
Strength: 145 tanks and 34 assault guns

3.SS.Panzergrenadier-Division *Totenkopf*

SS.*Brigadeführer* Priess
3.*SS.*Panzer-Regiment, 5.SS.Panzergrenadier-Regiment Thule, 6.*SS.*Panzergrenadier-Regiment *Theodor Eicke,* 3.*SS.*Panzer-Artillerie-Regiment, 3.*SS.*Panzer-Reconnaissance-Bataillon, 3.*SS.*Flak-Bataillon, 3.*SS.*Panzer-Engineer-Bataillon, 3.*SS.*Flak-Bataillon
Strength: 139 tanks and 35 assault guns

122.Artillerie-Kommand (Arko)

1.Feld-Howitzer-Detachment, 861.Artillerie-Regiment (mot); 1.Feld-Howitzer-Detachment, 3.Bataillon, 818.Artillerie-Regiment (mot); 3.Smoke-Truppen; 55.Werfer-Regiment; 1.Werfer-Lehr-Regiment

680.Pioneer-Regiment

627.Pioneer-Bataillon (mot), 666.Pioneer-Bataillon (mot)

Total Strength: 390 tanks and 104 assault guns

On 5 July 1943, as the *II.SS.Panzer-Korps* stood poised ready to go into action, the pre-dawn light was shattered by a massive German bombardment. The artillery barrage was so intense that in no less than one hour German gunners had hurled more shells than they had used in both Poland and the Western campaigns put together. Despite this violent bombardment, Soviet artillery responded with equal ferocity that soon confirmed what all Germans feared: the attack was not a surprise. All over the front, Soviet artillery crews fired at known German artillery positions that caught the German gunners in the open.

Within hours of the artillery bombardment, the three *Waffen-SS* divisions were engaged in the opening stages of the greatest armoured clash in history. The task of the *SS.Panzer-Korps* was to advance via Beresov and Sadeynoye, and break through the first defensive belt. Between Lutchki and Jakovlevo was the second line of Russian defensive positions, and when these were destroyed the advance would follow in a general north-eastern direction. For this operation the 167.*Infanterie*-Division would form part of the *SS Korps* and would guard the left flank.

The *Leibstandarte's* first attack went well, and their armour soon encircled enemy units that were destroyed with supporting grenadiers. The *9.Kompanie* of the *Leibstandarte's* 2.SS.Panzergrenadier-Regiment captured two hills west of Byelgorod and took five fortified positions with explosive charges. The soldiers of the *Totenkopf* division too wasted no time and smashed onto a series of strong Soviet defence lines. At the same time the *Das Reich* division made considerable progress, and infiltrated enemy lines in front of them.

By evening of the first day of the attack *Totenkopf,* with its new Tiger tanks leading the advance, had reached the second Russian defensive belt and managed to capture the village of Yakhontovo and take an important command post of the Soviet 69th Army. Both the *Leibstandarte* and *Das Reich* had done equally as well. With their Tigers and Panzer IV's they had penetrated some 13 miles into the Russian defences.

By 7 July, the advance of the *SS.Panzer-Korps* seemed more promising than ever. *Totenkopf* had managed to smash its way through more than 30 miles of Russian line, whilst the *Leibstandarte* and *Das Reich* were equally successful despite enduring bitter fighting. *SS* battle reports confirmed that given the amount of Soviet prisoners taken and the damage inflicted on their lines, it appeared that the *SS.Panzer-Korps* was poised on the edge of victory.

However, they had not even yet encountered the main enemy positions. The fact that they had advanced at such speed had enabled the Russians to take full advantage of attacking the *SS* flanks.

The initial phase of the Soviet defensive action at Kursk was often crude, messy and costly, but in a tactical and operational sense it achieved its objectives. During the days that followed the Red Army, despite continuing to incur huge losses in both men and weaponry, deprived the *SS* of even tactical superiority. Against these elite troops they constantly strengthened their defences through reinforcement, skilfully deploying mobile armour and anti-tank reserves to compensate for the high losses. Within days the Russians had managed to ground down many of the *Wehrmacht* units, including those in the *SS.Panzer-Korps*, and throw its offensive timetable completely off schedule. It was here on the blood-soaked plains at Kursk that for the first time in the war the Red Army had savagely contested every foot of ground and was finally on an equal footing. Through sheer weight of Soviet strength and stubborn combat along an ever-extending front, the German mobile units were finally being forced to a standstill.

On 9 July, the *SS.Panzer-Korps* renewed their offensive against very strong enemy forces. In the vicious battle that ensued, the *SS* received a series of sustained attacks, but fanatically held their ground. Although they were in danger of being cut-off and encircled, they received orders to push forward and attack Soviet troops northeast of Beregovoy. During the advance, *Das Reich* guarded the eastern flank of *Totenkopf* and *Leibstandarte*. En route it became embroiled in bitter fighting in a huge tank battle in the hills around Prokhorovka on 12 July. Here the Soviet 5th Guard and 5th Guard Tank Armies clashed with the powerful armoured *SS* units consequently resulting in the climax of Operation *Zitadelle*. Throughout the attack the professionalism and technical ability of the *SS* was second to none. During the heavy fighting *SS* troops were often able to turn the balance even when the Russians had overwhelming superiority in numbers. In spite of the losses the units were imbued with optimism and continued to deliver to the enemy heavy blows.

During the climax of the battle both the *Totenkopf* and *Leibstandarte* attacked, whilst *Das Reich* remained on the defensive, repelling a number of armour and infantry attacks. Although Russian losses in both men and equipment far exceeded the German, their losses could be replaced. German losses, however, except where armour could be recovered, were total. Within less than a week of *Zitadelle* being unleashed both sides had lost several hundred tanks and thousands of troops. While the Red Army was able to repair and replace its losses, the *SS* divisions had to struggle on with what they had left at their disposal. Constantly, the soldiers were being slowly ground down in a battle of attrition. The Russians had committed no less than seven corps, with more than 850 tanks and SU-85 assault guns. Wave upon wave of Russian T-34 tanks poured a storm of fire onto the *SS* positions. When the Soviet tanks run out of ammunition, the crews often physically rammed the German tanks. Dismounted tanks crews then set about destroying the Panzers on foot using all weapons at their disposal, including grenades and mines. A *Leibstandarte* history captured the ferocity of the fighting:

At 06.00 hours, there was an attack by a force of regimental size across the line Prochororowka-Petrovka. About fifty enemy tanks ran into *Panzergruppe* LAH, which was just beginning its advance. The fighting lasted two hours.

Unterstürmfuhrer Guehrs, the *Zugführer* of a *Kraftwagenkanonenzug* (armoured gun platoon) in the III. (Armoured)/2.Panzergrenadier-Regiment, reported as follows:

> They attacked us in the morning. They were around us, on top of us, and between us. We fought man-to-man, jumping out of foxholes to lob our magnetic hollow charge grenades at the enemy tanks, leaping on our *Schützenpanzerwagen's* to take on any enemy vehicle or man we spotted. It was hell!! At 09.00 hours, the battlefield was once again firmly in our hands. Our Panzers had helped us. My *Kompanie* alone had destroyed fifteen Russian tanks.[2]

Similar battles of attrition were fought in many parts of the *II.SS.Panzer-Korps*, but it was the soldiers of the *Leibstandarte* that were bearing the brunt of the fighting. Everywhere enemy troops charged the *SS* positions, turning these once mighty soldiers from attackers to desperate defenders. The division's 1.SS.Panzergrenadier-Regiment had no sooner attacked and captured an important position, when it was repeatedly struck by waves of Russian tanks and mounted infantry and compelled to go over to the defensive.

By 13 July, the *II.SS.Panzer-Korps* was unable to make any further progress, and poor ground conditions were hampering its re-supply efforts. As a consequence Russian forces managed to drive back the 3.Panzer-Division in the area of the Rakovo-Kruglik road and recaptured Hill 247, and the town of Berezovka. The following day, *Totenkopf* was forced out of its bridgehead on the northern bank of the Psel River, while further east *Das Reich* had made limited progress, capturing the town of Belenichino. The *Grossdeutschland* Division was ordered to attack westwards, in order to recapture the ground lost by the 3. Panzer Division. Following another day of bitter fighting the division finally managed to link up with 3. Panzer at Berezovka, but it was unable to dislodge Russian forces from Hill 247.

On 15 July, *Das Reich* made contact with the 7. Panzer-Division. However the Russian offensive to the north of the salient was now threatening the 9.*Armee* rear and it was forced to begin a planned withdrawal westwards to avoid encirclement. Following its withdrawal, almost all offensive action around Prokhorovka ceased and German forces in the area went over to the defensive.

By 17 July, a further series of Russian offensives opened along the entire Eastern Front. The *II. SS.Panzer-Korps* and the *Grossdeutschland* Division were withdrawn from 4. Panzer-Army, and the operation cancelled. By 23 July the 4.Panzer-Army had withdrawn to its start line.

Operation *Zitadelle* was a catastrophe for the German forces on the Eastern Front. Hitler had chosen an objective that was far too ambitious. The attack had also been continually delayed, allowing Russian forces additional time to prepare their defensive positions in the salient. Despite German efforts to batter their way through, they had neither the strength nor resources to do so. The cream of the German panzer force, so carefully concentrated prior to the operation, was exhausted and the Russians had undeniably gained the initiative in the East. The campaign in Russia would now consist of a series of German withdrawals with the *Waffen-SS* fanatically contesting every foot of the way.

Many German commanders openly blamed the second front in Italy for draining German forces on the Eastern Front, and believed that they failed when victory at Kursk was within their grasp. However, although it is true that the second front did drain vital resources from Russia, it would not have markedly improved its chances even if the second front had not begun, especially against an enemy of unrivalled strength. The Soviets at Kursk had undoubtedly delivered the *Wehrmacht* and *Waffen-SS* divisions a severe battering from which the German war effort was never to recover. The Germans had lost some thirty divisions, including seven Panzer divisions. According to official Soviet sources, as many as 49,822 German troops were killed or missing and the Germans had lost 1,614 tanks and self-propelled guns. As for the *SS* divisions, the *Leibstandarte, Das Reich* and *Totenkopf* had lost more than half their vehicles and taken massive casualties. Red Army troops, however, suffered much higher losses with some 177,847 being killed and injured. They also lost a staggering 2,586 tanks and self-propelled guns during the battle.

Operation *Zitadelle* had finally ended the myth of the German invincibility and was the first time that the *blitzkrieg* concept had failed. The tide of victory in the East had finally been turned. But even as *Zitadelle* was drawing to a bloody conclusion, the *II.SS.Panzer-Korps* was not there to see the end of the battle: the remnants of their exhausted and battered units had already been hurriedly ordered to pull out of the Kursk area to the relative calm and quiet of Kharkov to wait for new orders. Before the *Leibstandarte* departed for Italy it turned over all of its remaining armoured fighting vehicles to *Das Reich*. Both *Totenkopf* and *Das Reich* were detached from the *Leibstandarte* and redeployed in the Donetz Basin on 25 July 1943. As for the *Leibstandarte*, the division was withdrawn on 3 August. A strong, tough and reliable *SS* division had been needed in Italy to prevent the whole peninsula from falling into Allied hands. For the next three months the *Leibstandarte* spent its duration as Occupation Forces engaging periodically in anti-partisan operations in northern Italy and in Slovenia.

On the Eastern Front, the fighting had intensified. The Russians were determined not to allow the Germans any respite and launched a massive attack, overrunning *Feldmarschall* von Manstein's positions on the River Mius. Both *Totenkopf* and *Das Reich* were rushed north to protect Manstein's left flank.

The opening attack at Kursk on 5 July 1943. Here an armoured vehicle belonging to the 1.*SS. Leibstandarte* Panzer-Division moves towards the front towing an anti-tank gun.

Waffen-SS trainees successful enough to pass the very intensive training were rewarded with the passing out parade, where the *SS* oath was taken. Initially the candidates then had to spend a year in one of the *SS* infantry or cavalry schools, before returning to Munich to swear another oath of allegiance to Heinrich Himmler. The *SS* recruit was now an ordained *SS* soldier. He was an elite warrior, highly mobile, whose training programme had been rigorous and fanatical.

Soldiers belonging to the 5.*SS. Wiking Panzergrenadier-Division* are training prior to their deployment on the Eastern Front. Here a *SS* soldier prepares his MG 34 machine for live ammunition firing.

5.SS. Wiking recruits are being taught infantry assault techniques. Every instructor placed great emphasis on aggression and every possible means by which to overcome the enemy quickly and efficiently, with the least amount of friendly casualties. Unlike the Army, whose basic training was drill and more drill, *SS* training emphasised physical toughness and fighting skills.

5.SS. Wiking recruits are cleaning their weapons. The men had to practise on their own weapons, constantly repeating the disassembly and reassembly process until they could do it blindfolded.

Following the massive artillery bombardment on Russian positions at Kursk the *Waffen-SS* surged forward towards the heavily defended belts of mines, anti-tank guns, and well dug-in Red Army positions. Here a *Leibstandarte* Sd.Kfz.251 halftrack moves forward towards the burning Russian lines.

Soldiers of a *Leibstandarte* flak unit are preparing an 8.8cm flak gun to be used in anger against Russian ground positions during the first day of Operation *Zitadelle*. Painted on the rear of the halftrack is the unit symbol of the *Leibstandarte*. This marking was a white skeleton key painted at an angle inside a white shield. The key alluded to the name of the unit commander, Josef Sepp Dietrich, Sepp being the German word for key.

Grenadiers of the *Wiking* division hitch a lift on board a Pz.Kpfw.IV during the early days of the battle of Kursk in July 1943. Within hours of the opening attack the *SS.Panzer-Korps* divisions had smashed through the first Russian defensive belt with comparative ease and some daring feats of heroism were undertaken by a number of tank commanders.

One of the many Tiger tanks destined to take part at Kursk, here seen on a flatbed railway car. The use of the Tiger tank provided both the *Wehrmacht* and *Waffen-SS* with a dramatic improvement in the power of German armoured formations, both because of the real technical advantages of the Tiger, and propaganda advantages of creating elite units in the *Panzertruppen*.

The *SS* crew of a Pz.Kpfw.III pose for the camera wearing their distinctive black Panzer uniforms. The tank is on a railway flatcar destined for the front lines. The main factor of the success of the armoured formations in Russia was their speed and mobility and the ability to be quickly and efficiently transported from one sector of the front to another by rail transport.

A Sd.Kfz.251 halftrack passes a burning house during bitter fighting at Kursk in July 1943. The *Waffen-SS* acquired halftracks much later than the *Wehrmacht* - not until 1942, when Hitler decided to upgrade the *Leibstandarte, Das Reich*, and *Totenkopf* to full Panzergrenadier divisions in reward for sterling service in the East.

Waffen-SS grenadiers move forward during the early stages of Operation *Zitadelle*. The battlefield at Kursk was a huge agricultural plain of cornfields interspersed with belts of tall steppe grass, large open areas, broken by valleys and several rivers. The Germans regarded it as ideal tank country.

Waffen-SS grenadiers dressed in their familiar summer camouflage smocks wait inside a trench prior to going back into action during the Kursk offensive. From their starting positions the *SS* divisions covered a sector more than 12 miles wide. *Totenkopf* occupied the left flank of the thrust, while *Leibstandarte* moved along in the centre and *Das Reich* held the right.

Waffen-SS soldiers go on the offensive with an MG34 machine gun set up on a Dreifuss 34 anti-aircraft tripod mount. The firepower of the *SS* was one of the most important factors in overwhelming the Red Army throughout the entire war. When facing an *SS* machine gun team supplied with plenty of ammunition, Russian units frequently had trouble suppressing the weapon without suffering substantial losses themselves.

Another view of the same *Waffen-SS* machine gunner and his team within a fenced area of a Russian farmhouse. The MG34 provided the *SS* grenadiers with direct and indirect fire support necessary to prevail both on the attack and in defence.

2. Kharkov and Beyond

Following the failure of Operation *Zitadelle* German forces were now on the defensive. In the southern sector of the Eastern Front troops frantically withdrew as strong Russian forces smashed through the Mius defences and advanced at breakneck speed towards Stalino and Taganrog, along the northern coast of the Sea of Azov. Although *SS* troops of *Das Reich* and *Totenkopf* distinguished themselves with their bravery, they could only manage to stem the Red Army for short periods of time. Along the banks of the Mius River the *SS* had blunted Soviet forces and sent enemy units reeling back across the river. Such was the success of the *SS* that on 17 August 1943 *Das Reich* received a rare commendation from the commander of *Heeresgruppe Süd, Feldmarschall* von Manstein:

> In a daring and energetically led attack along the west flank of the army, the division has destroyed a considerable enemy force, and thus created the necessary condition for further operations. I convey to the division and its officers my special recognition. Mention of the division in the *Wehrmacht* communiqué has been approved.[1]

However, by mid-August 1943, the Russians had wrenched open a huge gap in the German lines west of Kursk, once again threatening to re-take the important industrial city of Kharkov. *Das Reich, Totenkopf* and *Wiking* divisions were immediately thrown into battle to prevent the loss of the city. Although all these combat formations were weakened by the *Zitadelle* disaster, they were still a formidable fighting force. The city itself had only been re-captured by the *Waffen-SS* in March 1943, and now it was the Red Army's turn to launch a massive pincer attack to capture it back again.

Within days of the *SS* redeployment to Kharkov the Russian 53rd Army driving from the north and the 57th Army advancing from the south, attacked the city with all its might. Almost immediately the *SS* troops crashed into action and defended Kharkov with every drop of blood.

On 20 August *Totenkopf* and the *Grossdeutschland* division joined hands to close the gap west of the city. However, by this stage of the battle both divisions were running out of ammunition and were already relying heavily on artillery to undertake the main burden of defending their positions. The high consumption of ammunition in the last month had put serious strain on all the German combat formations in and around Kharkov. In many units daily requirements in artillery and tank ammunition were down to half the normal capacity required to sustain a force of such magnitude in a defensive position. And yet, despite these problems, Manstein still thought he might be able to hold Kharkov by using *Das Reich* in a counterattack. The soldiers of *Das Reich* were to throw everything they could possibly muster against the Soviets. But when they arrived in the 6.*Korps* zone of operations, they found that the artillerymen, after firing their last rounds, were abandoning their guns and fighting as infantry.

Fighting around the city was heavy. In just one day fighting *SS* anti-tank gunners knocked out nearly 200 Soviet tanks. The *Das Reich* Panther battalion, which first saw heavy combat on the 22 August, destroyed 53 Russian tanks. The next day, just west of Kharkov, a Panther platoon broke up a Russian tank assault, and one Panther destroyed 7 tanks. On 24 August, the 6.*SS.Panzer-Kompanie* newly supplied with the latest Panzer IV's, battled 60 Russian T–34 tanks between Udy-Bogens and Orkan, just south-west of the city, and knocked out 29 of the 60 tanks. In the ten-day battle that raged around Kharkov the *Das Reich* division alone had scored 463 armoured kills.

Totenkopf and *Wiking* were equally as impressive, and fought a series of skilful duels against numerically superior enemy forces. Again and again they showed their worth in the field of action. In spite of serious losses in men and material, the troops continued fighting with all the ruthlessness and *élan* that made them such an efficient and lethal weapon of war.

Through the later part of August the *SS* continued to score some outstanding successes in localised combats with Russian armoured units. However, with acute shortages in men and equipment the situation deteriorated day by day. Despite frantic calls from commanders appealing for the evacuation from the city, Hitler sent out an order that Kharkov be held under all circumstances and demanded the most severe measures against any units that failed to execute their assigned missions. Instead, both *Wehrmacht* and *Waffen-SS* units were forced to undertake their *Führer's* futile exercise of holding Kharkov to the grim death.

However, as developments rapidly deteriorated and the hard-pressed soldiers became ground down against numerically superior forces, Hitler became increasingly worried that another Stalingrad would soon develop. By early September he grudgingly decided to go ahead and allow the order to pull the troops out of the doomed city. The evacuation of Kharkov was undertaken by a spirited withdrawal by the *Waffen-SS* towards the River Dnieper. Here the *SS* managed to halt the Russian onslaught towards the river, allowing Manstein's forces to retreat and re-deploy. Both *Totenkopf* and *Das Reich* had helped divert a major disaster in the area and given Manstein a little time to reorganise the front from the inevitable disaster that was looming. Both the *SS* divisions together with the elite arm of *Grossdeutschland* covered the general retreat to the river, before retiring themselves to the western bank of the river. Manstein was very aware that his army group could no longer hold the Donetz Line, and therefore sought to withdraw and regroup his forces across the River Dnieper. Altogether some sixty-eight German divisions – 1,250,000 men and over 2,000 tanks of *Heeresgruppe Süd* – were tasked with holding the river line at all costs. Opposing them, however, was a Red Army almost double in size, and furnished with plenty of reserves in fresh men and equipment.

The River Dnieper was the second largest Russian river and the strongest natural defence line in western Russia. Fortified and adequately manned, the Dnieper would have certainly been ideally defensible; but the condition of *Heeresgruppe Süd* in September 1943 was such that the river was only modestly capable of affording any natural protection and delaying the Soviet advance. When troops crossed the river during their withdrawal from Kharkov they were dismayed to find none of the impregnable fortifications constructed.

Here along the River Dnieper there was still no respite from the fury of the Russian advance. In the first ten days of October the Red Army launched an attack against German positions in the great bend of the river, between Kremenchug and Zaporozhye. The attack begun with a massive artillery preparation that pounded the German bridgehead. In no less than an hour the Germans had counted some 15,000 shell bursts in their sector. German batteries replied in kind as far as they were able, but the main attack would fall on the infantry. By 15 October, the Russian 2nd Ukrainian Front, with a total of six armies, bulldozed its way through and crossed the river. During the next few days they poured divisions across the river and tore open the German held front between the 8.*Armee* and the left wing of the *I. Panzer-Armee*. On 18 October troops took Pyatikhatka, thirty-five miles south of the Dnieper, and cut off the main railway lines to Dnepropetrovsk and Krivoi Rog. Russian forces were now driving straight for Krivoi Rog, the supply and communication centre for *Heeresgruppe Süd*. The city of Krivoi Rog contained the supply and ammunition dumps for the area, and the locomotives there were a vital asset for the supply to the army group.

Manstein was determined that he could not allow the loss of Krivoi Rog and scraped together what he could muster to the stem the Russian onslaught. He managed to find six weakened armoured divisions, including *Totenkopf*. Even the units of the *SS* were hard pressed and did not receive the ample supplies of fresh men and armour that they had been promised. Instead they were put into line on the right flank of the Soviet advance. What followed was a massive counter-thrust with *Wehrmacht* and *Waffen-SS* troops using all available reserves and resources to bitterly contest the Russian advance. In the bloody battle that ensued the Germans, at great cost in men and material, managed to break up two Russian armoured corps and nine rifle divisions. The Red Army lost more than 300 tanks and 5,000 prisoners. The remaining Russian forces in the area staggered back towards the Dnieper, allowing the exhausted German combat formations to temporarily stabilise the front.

The troops were made fully aware of the significance of holding the vital city of Krivoi Rog, and the outcome would be the deciding factor in the future operations of *Heeresgruppe Süd* in the Crimea.

Further north along the River Dnieper soldiers of *Das Reich* had meanwhile been trying to prevent large numbers of enemy forces from consolidating control areas west of the river. Both *SS* troopers and Red Army forces had been battling throughout late September and October, the Germans trying to stop the Russians establishing a bridgehead. The *Der Führer* regiment had seized the town of Grebeni, but at great cost. Only 500 soldiers were left in its ranks. Still undeterred from the losses, *Das Reich* continued to fight a number of inconclusive battles in the region, which saw its regiments and battalions become even further depleted.

Throughout the weeks that ominously followed the German front lines were pulled farther westwards with *Das Reich* defending, attacking and counter-attacking as the situation demanded. A number of the successful battles that were fought in this sector of the front were owed to the efforts of the *SS*, but they came with a high price in blood.

A *SS* Panzer commander poses for the camera next to his Pz.Kpfw.IV. The special black vehicle uniform for tank and armoured crews was developed from the existing Army equivalent. The uniform in this photograph is that of an *SS.Untersturmführer* of the *Leibstandarte*.

Grenadiers of the *Das Reich* division pose for the camera next to a light Horch cross-country vehicle. All the soldiers are wearing the familiar summer camouflage smocks and field cap. The soldier on the far left of the photograph holds the rank of an *SS Sturmann*.

SS troops with an anti-tank gun during operations with *Heeresgruppe Mitte* in 1943. These soldiers belong to the 8.*SS*.Kavallerie-Division *Florian Geyer*, which saw bitter fighting until it was transferred to *Heeresgruppe Süd* in July 1943.

Waffen-SS soldiers of a reconnaissance battalion with captured Soviet soldiers during heavy fighting south of Kursk in August or September 1943. There are two heavy armoured cars, including an Sd.Kfz.232 radio vehicle equipped with a frame antenna.

A group of soldiers belonging to the *Leibstandarte* take cover during bitter fighting south of Kiev in early November 1943. The soldiers are wearing reversible winter clothing, which allowed them to wear white or grey, depending on the season and weather conditions. Note how the constant wear has turned their normally white garments into a dirty grubby appearance.

A soldier belonging to the *Wiking* Division scours the terrain ahead, standing next to a stationary StuG.III. Ausf.G during operations in 1943. Throughout the war, especially during the last two years, assault guns and self-propelled guns proved indispensable to the *Waffen-SS* on the Eastern Front. During 1943 the *Leibstandarte, Das Reich, Totenkopf* and *Wiking* divisions were all equipped with assault gun battalions. They were later followed by *Nordland, Reichsführer-SS,* and the refitted *SS-Polizei* divisions, who all gained new assault gun battalions as well.

SS soldiers trying to deduce the location of the enemy through well-camouflaged scissor binoculars. By mid-1943 the Germans were on the defensive everywhere, but on the Eastern Front Hitler was optimistic that he could wrest the initiative away from the enemy with the aggressive spirit of his loyal *Waffen-SS*.

A *SS* machine gun crew move forward during operations in southern Russia in September 1943. As the Red Army began to take the initiative the Germans soon developed effective defensive tactics and techniques designed around the prowess of the MG 34 and MG 42 machine guns.

A variety of *SS* armoured vehicles spread out across the vast steppe of southern Russia during late summer operations of 1943. In late August 1943 Soviet forces began to advance, and the *Waffen-SS* took part in a fighting withdrawal towards the Dnieper.

Troops of the *Leibstandarte* division take cover during fighting along the Mius River in late July 1943. Two of the soldiers are wearing helmet netting in order to protect themselves against mosquitoes and other winged insects along the river.

Leibstandarte troops with their commanding officer inside a light cross-country Horch car, prior to the Division's posting to Italy. Following the *Leibstandarte's* failure at Kursk the division was reorganised and refitted in the Isyum area, where it re-entered the battle along the Mius river line until it was finally withdrawn on 3 August 1943.

SS engineers erecting a pontoon bridge across the Dnieper River in southern Russia in the late stages of the summer campaign with *Heeresgruppe Süd*. During September 1943 some 68 German divisions – 1,250,000 men and over 2000 tanks - were withdrawn across the Dnieper river and were tasked with holding the river line at all costs.

A *SS* MG 34 machine gunner of the *Leibstandarte* prepares to open fire. The MG 34 was widely used by the *Waffen-SS* throughout the war. The gun enjoyed a solid and rugged design that had a tremendous fire rate of up to 1550 rounds per minute.

A *SS* MG 34 machine gun crew in action in November 1943. The machine gun is on a Dreifuss anti-aircraft tripod mounting. With this powerful weapon *SS* troops were aware that they had considerable defensive staying power against enemy infantry as long as they could keep their machine gun operational and deployed with good fields of fire.

Vehicles laden with *SS* troops move along a forested road passing a flak gun and crew. The flak gun has been more than likely deployed in order to try and protect the column of vehicles from aerial attack as its forces withdraw to a new defensive line.

SS soldiers marching in two columns on either side of a dirt road in northern Russia in early October 1943. By this period of the war German forces were being gradually driven back by the gathering momentum of the Red Army.

3. Fighting Withdrawal

As the winter of 1943 approached, a feeling of despair and gloom gripped the German front lines. To many of the soldiers there was a dull conviction that the war was lost, and yet there was still no sight of its end. Being always outnumbered, perpetually short of fuel and ammunition, and having to constantly exert themselves and their machinery to the very limits of endurance had a profound effect on life at the front. During the later half of 1943 the equipment situation continued to deteriorate, especially in the Panzer units. The effect of starving the experienced and elite formations like the *Waffen-SS* was a constant concern for the tacticians. The *SS* did receive a high proportion of tanks, artillery and assault guns, but this was in stark contrast to the enormous volume of armaments being produced by the Russians. The *SS* were thus faced with a dangerous and worsening prospect, but unlike the normal German soldier many of these elite troops retained their fanatical determination on the battlefield. Against the growing Soviet menace they still proved to be first class formations. Their new role as the so-called fire brigades, being shuttled from one danger spot to another to dampen down heavy Russian attacks, typified their position during late 1943. In total there were seven SS divisions that became Hitler's emergency fire brigade, and it was in October 1943 that these seven crack *SS.Panzergrenadier* Divisions – *Leibstandarte Adolf Hitler, Das Reich, Totenkopf, Wiking, Hohenstaufen, Frundsberg,* and *Hitlerjugend* – were redesignated *SS* Panzer divisions.

The seven new divisions maintained and enhanced the military reputation of the *Waffen-SS*. As the *Wehrmacht* established defensive lines in the face of the advancing enemy, commanders looked at the aggressive and loyal striking force of the *SS* to be counted upon to snatch victory from defeat. It was for this reason that Hitler was forced to order the return of the *Leibstandarte* from Italy. By November 1943, barely three months after departing, the division now completely rested, and re-equipped with the latest tanks and assault guns returned to its old fighting ground in the East.

The *SS* division arrived on the battlefield south of Kiev in early November 1943. It was to be the main attacking division alongside the 4.Panzer-Division and was to strike northwards towards Kiev, which had already fallen into enemy hands. When the attack opened on 13 November the *Leibstandarte* formed two *Kampfgruppen*. The left arm went via Rogosna, crossed the Kamenka and Unova rivers and cut the Fastov-Brodel railway line south of Mochnachka. The right group drove north-eastwards, passed Pistachki, captured Trylissi, then established bridgeheads across the Kamenka river, and then drove with all its might towards Festov. It was here at Festov that the first major tank battles of the offensive were unleashed. The new Panzer ace, *SS.Obersturmführer* Michael Wittmann, destroyed six Soviet tanks and five anti-tank guns before driving to the rear echelon to refuel and take on more ammunition. Returning to battle following lunch he then destroyed a further ten tanks and another seven guns. *SS* grenadiers were then able to reach the Kiev-Zhitomir highway. The town of Brusilov was then captured and the *SS* advance temporarily continued. Inevitably though, the *SS* Panzer thrusts soon slowed and then halted. Operations in the area ceased on 23 November, when warm weather turned the roads into a quagmire.

In the *Das Reich* area of operations the division also fought well and with distinction to contain the Russians from marching across the western Ukraine. However, the unrelenting fighting had proven to be more than even *Das Reich* could endure. Consequently, by December 1943, it was no longer capable of carrying out the tasks given to a full-strength division and orders were issued to create a *Kampfgruppe* from the units still fit for action. On 17 December the Panzer *Kampfgruppe* was constructed out of the Panzergrenadier-Regiment *Das Reich*. The *Kampfgruppe* consisted of the 1.*Bataillon Deutschland* and 2.*Bataillon Der Führer Regiments*. Two companies constituted the Panzer battalion *Das Reich*, and also on strength were the reconnaissance battalion, artillery, *Nebelwerfers*, pioneers, a heavy infantry gun company and two self-propelled companies. The strength of *Kampfgruppe Das Reich*, as it was now called, would remain on the Eastern Front while the remaining elements returned to Germany for a refit.

Whilst *Kampfgruppe Das Reich* dug-in around the deep woods south-east of Radomyshl-Guta Sabelozkaya, near Krivoi Rog the *Totenkopf* division also continued attempting to hold vital ground against strong Russian forces. Although the division never regained the strength that it had possessed before *Zitadelle*, it had received more replacements in men and equipment than most of the divisions. Part of its success in the southern sector of the front was down to the fact that it was stronger than most of the formations that fought around it. The *Totenkopf* contained three full battalions of Panzergrenadiers, one weak battalion of tanks with about half of its normal establishment, and over half its normal artillery and flak. With this strength it managed to successfully halt the Soviet advance in mid-November. The division then dug-in and prepared its units for another Russian assault. What followed was a battle that raged for almost three days, during which time *Totenkopf* destroyed a staggering 247 Russian tanks. However, *Totenkopf's* success was shortly lived.

On 25 November the Red Army once again attacked its positions, and for three days and nights the division endured one of the fiercest attacks in its history as an *SS* combat formation. In no less than ten-days the Soviets once again renewed their offensive, smashed into the 384.Division and bulldozed past the left flank of the *I. Panzer-Armee*. On 6 December the Russian flanks broke into open country and threatened Krivoi Rog from the northwest. As one of the crack 'fire brigade' divisions the *Totenkopf* was ordered to be rushed to the crisis sector and once again displayed its skill and tenacity on the battlefield. Whilst the *SS* troops held the Russian forces in check, on 19 December the 11. and 13.Panzer divisions were moved forward and launched a major counterattack, with the *Totenkopf* leading the drive. The counterattack once again restored the area from the clutches of the Red Army and the town of Krivoi Rog was in German hands. The desperate defence by the *Totenkopf* and its fellow divisions had bought enough time to remove the bulk of the supplies, ammunition, vehicles and rolling stock from the area that would have been irretrievably lost if the Russians had reached Krivoi Rog sooner.

Following the successful German counteroffensive a short-lived optimism prevailed through the soldiers of *Heeresgruppe Süd*. Red Army troops that had been taken prisoner were either young boys or old men. Throughout the ranks hope began to grow that maybe now the Soviets had begun to exhaust their huge reserves of manpower and that the war might be finally being fought on equal terms. However, these thoughts were soon put to rest when on Christmas Eve 1943, the Russians in the southern sector of the front, renewed their westward push with all the power and ferocity that symbolised Soviet battle tactics in the last two years of the war. The Red Army soon engulfed its powerful infantry and armoured divisions around Kiev and quickly recaptured Zhitomir. Although Manstein's forces slowed the enemy onslaught, many German units had already been pushed back some 100 miles. Their fighting withdrawal had proven to be successful, but was a temporary measure. Technically it was a slow painful retreat that was rapidly spiralling out of control, draining all available German reserves and resources. As for the *Waffen-SS* during the withdrawal, they continued to prove a formidable and ruthless fighting machine – halting and rolling back the Russian advance and effectively helping to prevent the ultimate collapse of *Heeresgruppe Süd*.

Two *SS* soldiers pose for the camera standing next to their Sd.Kfz.221 light four-wheeled armoured car. The armoured car not only provide the mobility that was crucial to success, it became synonymous with the daring ethos of the *Waffen-SS*.

Troops of the *estnische Waffengrenadier*-Division der *SS* move towards the front in a halftrack towing a Pak gun in the summer of 1943. This foreign *SS* division was made-up mainly of Estonian soldiers and fought extensively in northern Russia until the end of the war.

Artillerymen of the *SS-Polizei-Division* in the winter of 1943. The division saw severe action in *Heeresgruppe Nord* in the Ladoga area until March 1943, until the front finally stabilised. Parts of the division were withdrawn from the line in October and sent to training areas in Bohemia, Moravia and Silesia. A small part of the division remained in Russia and was designated as *Kampfgruppe SS-Polizei-Division.*

Soldiers of the *SS* Flak Abteilung of the *SS-Polizei-Division* prepare to use their flak gun in anger against Russian positions in the winter of 1943. Throughout its active service in *Heeresgruppe Nord* the divisional records noted that the *SS.Polizei* was frequently cited for its excellent and responsive fire support.

A flak gun mounted on a Sd.Kfz.7 halftrack in the winter of 1943. By the end of 1943 mechanised *Waffen-SS* formations had become well-equipped with flak guns. Apart from a five battery motorised flak battalion, divisions also had additional anti-aircraft platoons and companies in their Panzergrenadier, Panzer and artillery regiments.

A gun crew from an unidentified *SS-Polizei-Division* artillery unit pose for the camera in a hastily-prepared dug out on Christmas Day, 1943. One of the crewmembers can be seen holding a bottle of schnapps, preparing to toast the day with his comrades.

At the moment of firing a *SS* artillery crew can be seen in action with a 10.5cm le. FH18 howitzer. In total, the 10.5cm howitzer had a nine-man crew. Four of its crewmembers can be seen here.

SS troops in the depth of the Russian winter of late 1943 utilise blocks of snow for a defensive position. Between mid-November and the end of the year, both the *Leibstandarte* and *Das Reich* took part in a number of counterattacks, but were unable to stem the Russian advance.

Wehrmacht and *Waffen-SS* troops withdrawing together from the Red Army onslaught in November 1943. The road has been churned into a morass making the withdrawal more difficult for wheeled transport.

A machine gun crew of the *Nord* division in late 1943. These snow troopers are wearing the shapeless two-piece snowsuit consisting of a white jacket and white trousers. With Red Army forces wearing similar clothing, frontline German troops were issued with coloured arm bands for use on their winter clothing. These enabled them to distinguish between friend and foe.

A *SS* MG 34 machine gunner and his number two during winter fighting in 1943. The German war on the Eastern Front, especially during retrograde movements, owed much to the *SS* machine gun infantry squads that were able to continue resistance after suffering losses that would have rendered enemy infantry ineffective.

Throughout the war in the East, especially during the autumn and spring months, vehicles continuously became bogged down in the seemingly bottomless Russian mud. Roads were few, and cross-country travel caused its own problems. Even during the withdrawal of late 1943 the Russian weather offered the Germans considerably greater challenges than they had faced in any other theatre of war. Here in this photograph an 8.8cm flak crew struggle to manoeuvre their weapon and tracked vehicle through the mire.

A brief respite for four *Das Reich* soldiers, who have taken shelter behind a knocked-out Russian T-34 tank. By early November 1943, the *Das Reich* division had been ground down to a fraction of its former size. Much of the shattered remnants were withdrawn to France while a nucleus of the division remained active in the East as *Kampfgruppe Lammerding*.

A *SS* MG 34 machine gunner scours the snow-covered terrain. Throughout the war *Waffen-SS* grenadiers took great pains to deploy their machine guns in the most advantageous defensive positions and employed elaborate camouflage to conceal them.

Leibstandarte troops with a light 7.5cm Infantry Gun 18 during winter operations in November 1943. Although the Infantry Gun 18 was regarded by the *SS* as an antiquated weapon, critical shortages had led them to use every available item that they could muster in order to try and stem the Soviet onslaught.

PART II

Combat Deployment in the East Winter 1943-Summer 1944

4. Southern Front

In early January 1944, Manstein's *Heeresgruppe Süd* had fallen back to the Panther-Wotan Line, a defensive position along the Dnieper River. At this point strong Soviet forces attempted to smash German forces around the town of Kirovograd. By 8 January the town fell, but the Russians soon found German resistance in the area stronger than expected. Some eleven German divisions, including the *SS Wiking* division and the new Belgian Walloon volunteer unit, *SS Sturmbrigade Wallonien*, which had recently been transferred from the *Wehrmacht* to *SS* control, were embroiled in a drastic attempt to stem the Soviet push westwards. Here these strong German divisions held a salient into the Soviet lines between the towns of Korsun and Cherkassy. Despite repeated warnings from Manstein, Hitler refused to allow the exposed units to be pulled back to safety.

On 18 January, Manstein was proven right when General Nikolai Vatutin's 1st and General Ivan Konev's 2nd Ukrainian Front's attacked the forward lines of the salient and surrounded two German corps. Trapped in the Korsun pocket were some 50,000 men, a total of six German divisions, including the elite *SS Wiking* and the *SS Sturmbrigade Wallonien*. The trapped forces were designated *Gruppe Stemmerman*, after its commander. The *Wiking* division had some 43 tanks and assault guns. Two assault gun battalions provided an additional 27 assault guns. *Wiking* was the only armoured unit in the pocket, and with these tanks and assault guns they were ordered to drive the enemy back and transform an impossible effort by breaking out of the encirclement and destroying the enemy. Day and night the fighting raged, but the Russians, with some thirty-five divisions around the salient, inflicted terrible casualties. The constant pressure gradually saw the pocket shrink to some 40 square miles by early February.

As disaster loomed a relief effort was quickly assembled. The 1. *SS.Panzer-Division Leibstandarte* was hurried to the area. *Oberstleutnant* Franz Bake's Tiger tanks of the 503.*Schwere-Panzer-Abteilung*, was ordered to help wrench open the pocket. However, the Tiger tanks and supporting vehicles found the terrain which they advanced very difficult. An unseasonable rise in temperature had caused a sudden thaw and turned the terrain into a boggy morass, making movement almost impossible in some areas. Nevertheless, deep in mud the *SS* pushed forward, and by 8 February elements of the *Leibstandarte* and 16.Panzer-Division had reached and established bridgeheads across the Gniloi Tickich River, west of Boyarka. *Gruppe Stemmerman* begun immediately pulling back troops from the north of the *Kassel*, and attacking south to expand towards the relief forces on the north bank of the Gniloi Tickich.

By 13 February the spearheads of the division were within grasp of the encircled troops, but were exhausted by their efforts, and ground to a halt on the line Lysanka – Oktyar – Chisinzy. Whilst the *Leibstandarte* battled slowly forward, Hitler at last consented to the evacuation of the Korsun pocket. On the night of 16 February, *Gruppe Stemmerman* received a communiqué from Manstein ordering it to breakout of the pocket at all costs. As *Wehrmacht* and *SS* troops begun to move slowly across the boggy terrain the Russians quickly became aware what was happening and opened up a massive barrage. Hundreds of Russian guns of all calibres poured a storm of fire on to the German positions. A *Wiking* soldier wrote later:

The most fearsome sound of all came from the *Katushkas* or Stalin Organs. These rocket machines with their distinctive shriek fired projectiles from 16-rail launcher is miles into the enemy lines. Although it was not a precision weapon, it

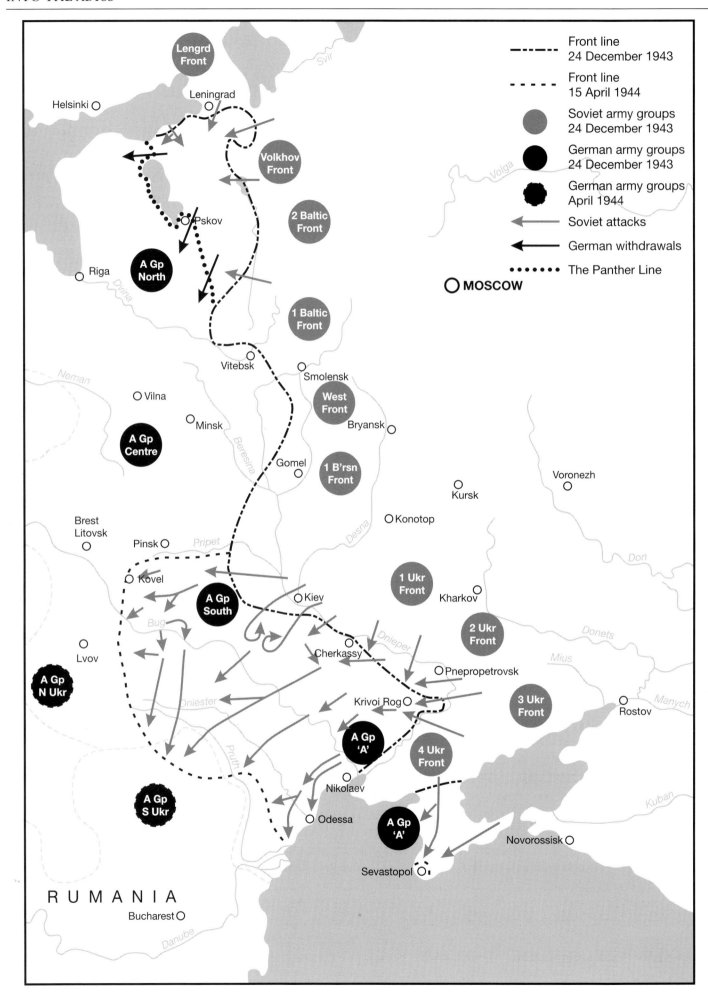

Map 2: Eastern Front, further German withdrawals December 1943-May 1944

was hardly necessary if 16 of them impacted in the same area. The terrifying noise they made was much feared by us, and the death and devastation they inflicted was terrible.[1]

Death and destruction inside the pocket was so severe that the wounded had to be left behind, as did most of the artillery and heavy equipment. *SS Sturmbrigade Wallonien* suffered terrible losses covering the rearguard, with almost three-quarters of its entire strength left dead on the battlefield. As the remnants pushed slowly forward nearer to the German lines, Russian fire intensified, inflicting even more casualties. In typical *Waffen-SS* style, the *Wiking* division's only remaining tanks turned back and fought to the death whilst the last of the brigade reached the German lines, before being overrun. The *SS Das Reich* too was another combat formation that had been rushed to help relieve the troops in the pocket. They were among the rearguard units, holding fast while the bulk of the encircled troops made good their escape. *Das Reich* had suffered heavy losses as a result of their self-sacrifice. Out of 5,000 soldiers that were sent to the area some 1,121 of all ranks were killed in action.

In spite of the huge losses in men and equipment, some 33,000 German troops had escaped with their lives. Another major disaster had been averted in southern Russia. The distinguished performances of the *Waffen-SS* had once again further increased its reputation as the foremost fighting machine on the Eastern Front. The *Wiking* commander Herbert Otto Gille and *SS-Hauptsturmführer* Leon Degrelle, commander of the *Walloons*, were summoned to Hitler's East Prussian headquarters, *Wolfsschanze*, and decorated. Gille received the Oakleaves and Swords, and Degrelle the Knight's Cross.

Following the breakout in the Korsun pocket the *Das Reich* Division, now totally depleted with most of its armour lost in the battle, was withdrawn from the front and sent to France for rest and refitting. A *Kampfgruppe* from the *Das Reich* division, under the command of *SS-Oberführer* Heinz Lammerding, remained in southern Russia to continue German attempts to try and hold back the Red Army.

During March 1944, *Heeresgruppe Süd* was forced to make a slow fighting withdrawal to the Dniester River, on the border with Romania. On 11 March, parts of the *Totenkopf* division that had been fighting fanatically as it pulled back towards the Dniester, was airlifted to Balta to form the core of a new defensive position there. As the Russians resumed their offensive towards the Dniester the *Das Reich Kampfgruppe*, shattered from weeks of intensive combat, continued doggedly to defend every foot of ground. All along the battered front lines there was no respite. The Soviet offensive tore a massive hole between the 1. and 4.Panzer-*Armee's* at Proskurov. Before the gap could be successfully sealed, the entire 1.Panzer-*Armee* found itself totally encircled in a huge pocket near the town of Kamenets-Podolsk. Among the units trapped were the *Das Reich Kampfgruppe* and the *Leibstandarte*. In the long fierce battle that ensued *Das Reich* recaptured the town of Isyaslavl and stemmed the Red Army drive. Fighting around the town raged until 14 March, until which time losses to the battered grenadier companies had become so severe that they could no longer hold their lines. As the situation deteriorated further across the whole area panicked stricken front line commanders pleaded for the release of the last *Waffen-SS* reserves to restore the situation. At this point Hitler agreed and allowed at once for the *II.SS.Panzer-Korps*, which consisted of the 9.SS.Panzer-Division *Hohenstaufen* and the 10.SS.Panzer-Division *Frundsberg*, to be rushed to the Eastern Front from France. Both *Hohenstaufen* and *Frundsberg* had been trained for nearly a year and equipped to a high standard and consisted mainly of *Reichsdeutsche* Germans. The soldiers were regarded as crack *SS*, and the basis of the divisions had been built around a cadre of personnel from units such as the *Leibstandarte* and *Das Reich*.

Whilst *Hohenstaufen* and *Frundsberg* boarded the long trains bound for southern Russia, Manstein's forces were being slowly bled to death inside the Kamenets-Podolsk Pocket. Tons of ammunition and fuel was being hurriedly airlifted into the pocket in order to avoid Manstein from abandoning all his heavy equipment and armour when the time came to breakout. When the two new *SS* divisions arrived in southern Russia they quickly launched a flank attack that smashed onto the tip of the Russian spearhead and allowed the trapped 1.Panzer-*Armee* to escape the slaughter. As the 1.Panzer-*Armee* fought its way out towards the west, the entire *SS* force joined arms and counterattacked in a relentless battle to take the pressure off the retreating Panzer army. It seemed that the *Waffen-SS* had once again averted another Stalingrad.

Immediately after their rescue in April 1944, *Hohenstaufen* and *Frundsberg* were withdrawn to Poland to prevent a renewal of the Red Army advance, but Hitler stipulated that these divisions would be called upon if there was an Allied invasion of northern Europe. As for the *Leibstandarte* and the *Das Reich Kampfgruppe*, they were withdrawn also from the front, but sent to the West for resting and refitting. Out of the 2,500 soldiers of the *Das Reich Kampfgruppe* only around 800 soldiers reached Toulouse in the southwest of France and rejoined the rest of their division. As for the *Leibstandarte*, the once fresh, well equipped, elite division that had entered the battlefields of southern Russia six months earlier, was now a battered and torn remnant of its former self. The remains of this powerful division, which consisted of a cadre of battle hardened *SS* veterans, were loaded on trains to begin their move westwards to Belgium and to prepare for the expected Allied invasion of northern France.

In the meanwhile, the remnants of the elite *SS Wiking* division was reformed into a 4,000 strong *Kampfgruppe* and hastily sent back to the battlefield, whilst the remainder were moved to Poland to be rebuild its once powerful division. As for the other SS divisions, *Totenkopf* continued in its year-long battle in southern Russia, trying with unabated ferocity to stem the colossus of the Soviet army. Already the Russian advance in the south had brought its armies perilously close to the borders of Hungary. Before panic had spread across the Southern Front, Hitler had ordered Operation *Margarethe* – the German occupation of Hungary. The operation was largely a *Waffen-SS* affair and consisted of second rate *SS* combat formations being used as fire brigade units. By April 1944, the 16.*SS*.Panzergrenadier-Division *Reichsführer-SS*, the 18.*SS*.Panzergrenadier-Division *Horst Wessel*, and the 8.*SS*.*Kavallerie*-Division *Florian Geyer* had taken up positions in Hungary.

Soldiers of the *Wiking* division pose for the camera next to what appears to be a food store containing loaves of bread. It is more than likely that these troops are temporarily guarding the store.

A group of *Waffen-SS* soldiers pose for the camera inside a forest clearing on the Eastern Front. Most of the troops are wearing the familiar oakleaf pattern camouflage smocks with its autumn/winter side exposed.

Two *Das Reich* soldiers wearing winter clothing scour the terrain ahead during a lull in the fighting in the area around the town of Cherkassy in late January 1944.

SS troops are preparing to disembark from a Pz.Kpfw.IV Ausf.G from a flatbed railway car during operations in southern Russia in late January 1944. The Panzer has received a coating of winter whitewash paint and *Zimmerit* anti-magnetic mine paste can clearly be seen applied to the vehicle's armour.

Various armoured vehicles of the *Waffen-SS* near Kirovgrad in January 1944. The vehicles have been purposely spaced out across the frozen plain in order to make it more difficult for Russian fighters to attack.

A Panzer crewman belonging to the *Leibstandarte* Panzer regiment stands in front of his Pz.Kpfw.IV Ausf.G during winter operations in southern Russia in January 1944. This photograph was taken just prior to the division spearheading an attack from the Vinnitsa area against the Red Army.

A Panzer crew belonging to the *Leibstandarte* Panzer regiment pose for the camera on board their whitewashed Pz.Kpfw.IV during the Division's drive near Vinnitsa in late January 1944.

A MG 34 machine gun crew belonging to the *Sturmbrigade Wallonien* defends just one of a number of positions against strong Russian attacks near Cherkassy in late January 1944. During the battle around Cherkassy the *Sturmbrigade Wallonien* suffered dreadful losses as it covered the rearguard, with 70 percent of its strength left dead in the snow.

Supplies have been dropped by the *Luftwaffe* to re-supply the beleaguered divisions trapped in the area around Cherkassy in early February 1944. Constant pressure from the Red Army eventually saw the salient shrink, until it measured some 40 square miles by 9 February.

Conditions in southern Russia in early 1944 for both the *Wehrmacht* and *Waffen-SS* were very grim. This photograph vividly illustrates the type of terrain that the soldiers fought across against overwhelming opposition. Scissor binoculars have been erected just clear of a very well-concealed underground bunker. A SS soldier can be seen in a trench surrounded by weapons protected from the arctic weather beneath tarpaulin.

A *SS* soldier stands between a support vehicle and a 7.5cm Pak 40 anti-tank gun in early 1944. In service the 7.5 cm Pak 40 proved a powerful and deadly weapon and became the most prolific German anti-tank gun of the war. Throughout the war, especially during the last two years, *Waffen-SS* gunners demonstrated the efficacy of the weapon in a number of defensive battles in the East.

Remaining Panthers of the *Das Reich* Division near Zhitomir in January 1944. The *Das Reich* Division was one of the first *Waffen-SS* divisions to re-equip with an entire battalion of Panther tanks. However, by January 1944, this battered division had lost all its original 49 Panthers during sustained action around Zhitomir.

Soldiers belonging to the *Das Reich Kampfgruppe Lammerding* during fierce winter fighting in January 1944 near the town of Zhitomir. Here the *SS* troops were constantly under pressure from the enemy and eventually forced to retreat westwards from the town through deep snowdrifts. During the day they fought, and by night the units marched.

Leibstandarte troops during a lull in the Division's advance towards Ninograd in early February 1944. Conditions in the area were very poor, but the frozen ground was sufficient to take the heavy tanks of the division, which formed the spearhead of the advance.

A StuG.III Ausf.G moves along a muddy road in southern Russia in early 1944. With the growing shortages of Panzers and delayed production of tank destroyers, the Germans were compelled by 1944 to integrate assault gun battalions into individual Panzer regiments and Panzerjäger battalions, where the StuG.III served until the end of the war.

Soldiers of the *Das Reich Kampfgruppe Lammerding* are trying to pull a vehicle out of the mud during operations in southern Russia in February 1944. Draped on the vehicles bonnet is the national flag used for aerial recognition.

SS troops being resupplied by *Luftwaffe* drops somewhere in the Cherkassy Pocket region in February 1944.

A Panther of the *Das Reich* Division partially conceals itself behind snow and foliage on the southern front in early 1944. With the Panthers, the *Waffen-SS* tank crews dominated the battlefields of the latter half of the war. But though they destroyed many enemy tanks, they were never available in sufficient numbers to alter the course of the war.

SS troops utilizing a sled through a forest during fierce fighting in the Cherkassy Pocket in February 1944. By this period of the war the *Waffen-SS* were well suited for winter warfare, having been provided with ample supplies of winter clothing.

The majority of these *SS* ski-troops are wearing white camouflage smocks. One soldier is armed with a MP 38/40 sub-machine gun. Ski troops were particularly effective against enemy formations, appearing suddenly out of the snow to sweep across a trench line, and attacking with weapons at the ready.

SS officers confer in a forest clearing during operations in southern Russia in early 1944. The soldier on the right, who holds the rank of an *SS-Unterscharführer*, has been awarded with an infantry assault badge.

SS soldiers during a lull in the fighting in southern Russia. By March 1944 the *Waffen-SS* were compelled to make a gradual withdrawal to the Dniester River, in spite of the huge sacrifices their forces had made trying to contain the Soviet forces.

During the withdrawal to the Dniester River *SS* troops stretcher one of the many wounded soldiers to a hastily-erected field hospital.

Commanding officers confer inside an aircraft hanger. The officer on the right who holds the rank of *SS-Untersturmführer* is wearing the M1944 herringbone camouflage uniform. This pea pattern camouflage suit is worn over his grey service uniform.

SS officers greet each other with smiles following a successful localised counterattack during one of the many winter battles that raged on the southern front in early 1944. Between January and March the *Waffen-SS* had managed to score a number of successful breakthroughs against strong Red Army forces, but due the enemy superiority were unable to retain their positions for any appreciable length of time.

Troops and motorcycle combination belonging to the *Leibstandarte*. This photograph was taken just prior to the Division's removal from the Eastern Front for a rest and refit westwards to Belgium in March 1944. The motorcycle combination still retains the old divisional insignia.

Totenkopf troops have rounded up Russian prisoners following the Division's fierce counter-offensive in the area around Kirovograd in March 1944.

Totenkopf officers joke amongst themselves during a lull in the fighting along defensive lines not far from the western borders of the Soviet Union in March 1944.

Totenkopf troops move across snow-covered terrain whilst acting as a rearguard for the 8.Armee. The winter and spring of 1944 was characterised by a series of constant withdrawals from one natural barrier to another in the face of constant massive Soviet offensives, which had slowly pushed the Germans back towards the western borders of the Soviet Union.

A MG 34 machine gun crew belonging to the *Das Reich* Division defends an edge of a forest against Russian infantry attacks in early February 1944. By this period of the fighting *Das Reich* was worn down by constant battles and heavy losses.

A *Totenkopf* 10.5cm field howitzer crew at dawn on the Eastern Front in March 1944. The 10.5cm leFH 18 light field howitzer had remained the standard light divisional howitzer throughout the war, and although it had insufficient mobility it provided the *Waffen-SS* with much of the firepower needed to sustain itself in defence on the battlefield.

5. Northern Front

In *Heeresgruppe Nord* the military situation was far worst than in the south. German forces were reeling back across a scarred and devastated wasteland of the northern front. By mid-January 1944 the Red Army had lifted the siege of Leningrad, had gone onto the offensive and was slowly but inexorably driving the German forces westwards towards the Baltic states of Estonia and Latvia. It was in this sector that most of the *Waffen-SS* volunteer divisions were deployed to try and stem the Soviet drive. The main *Waffen-SS* force in the area was *SS.Grupppenführer* Felix Steiner's III *Germanic Panzer-Korps*, the 11.*SS*.Freiwilligen-Division *Nordland* and *SS*.Freiwilligen Brigade *Nederland*. In addition to these volunteer divisions were the 15. and 19. *Waffengrenadier* divisions from Estonia, as well as the Flemish *Langemarck* Brigade and the Walloon Sturmbrigade *Wallonien*.

Although regarded as second-rate *SS* divisions these troops were formidable opponents. But despite their best efforts nothing could not mask the fact that they were dwarfed by the superiority of the Red Army. It was estimated that the Russians had some two million men on the northern front alone. To the *SS* volunteer soldier facing the might of the enemy, the outcome was almost certain death. The realisation among these men that they might be fighting a loosing battle was seldom admitted openly. Most of them already knew that the end would come soon. They were not convinced by their commander's encouragements, especially when they were lying in their trenches subjected to hours of bombardments by guns that never seemed to lack shells. Out on the battlefield these volunteer forces were urged on, not to fight and do their duty for the *Führer*, but to defend their land against the advancing Red Army.

During the second half of January the Russians had ploughed its way westwards, and by the end of the month had reached German fortified positions at the city of Narva. This German defensive line with hundreds of dug-in artillery positions and machine-gun nests ran from the city south along the banks of the River Narva, to the shores of Lake Peipus and down to Polotsk, northwest of Vitebsk. On the west bank of the River Narva *SS* units had constructed heavily defended emplacements. Here the soldiers of *Nordland* and *Nederland* were determined to stand firm and fight in what became known as the Battle of the European SS.

The main brunt of the Soviet attack was to fall on Steiner's *SS.Korps*, positioned east of Narva. On 3 February, the Soviet assault was finally unleashed and a bloody battle ensued. Almost immediately a Russian armoured group quickly penetrated the German line and established a bridgehead on the western bank of the Narva. The *Nordland's* Panzer *Abteilung*, named *Hermann von Salza*, and commanded by *SS-Obersturmbannführer* Paul Albert Kausch and assisted by Tiger ace *Leutnant* Otto Carius, and a platoon of four Tigers, crashed into action. Quickly eliminating the Soviet armour, the Panzers and Tigers then began supporting the *SS*-Grenadiers as they cleaned out the Soviet infantry. Although the crisis was temporarily averted in the centre, further north Red Army forces successfully established a bridgehead near the village of Siivertsi. To the south of the city of Narva, in the zone defended by an ad-hoc army *Abteilung* named *Narwa*, Russian soldiers crossed the river and threatened to cut off Steiner's *SS Korps* and two *Wehrmacht* units. The *502.Schwere Panzer-Abteilung* was moved into the threatened area and quickly stabilised the German line. To strengthen the German defence, the newly formed Estonian 20. *Waffengrenadier-Division der SS* (*Estnische Nr.1*) division was rushed into the line and attached to Steiner's *Korps*. Steiner threw the division into battle on 20 February against the Siivertsi bridgehead. The Estonian *SS* soon proved themselves in combat, and within nine days of continuous fighting Red Army troops had been pushed back across the river.

To the south, however, the German combat formations were collapsing under a fresh Soviet assault. By 24 February the Russian spearheads had reached the main rail line supplying the Narva area, and threatened to encircle Steiner's *Korps* to the north. Despite heavy resistance the Red Army pushed forward using heavy artillery and armour to smash through the German defenses. *Armee-Abteilung Narwa* rushed forces south to halt the Soviet advance. A battalion from the *Nordland's* 26. *SS*-Panzergrenadier Regiment *Norge* was also brought south to help bolster the disintigrating line.

Despite sustaining massive losses and being repelled a number of times, the Russians persistently attacked all across the Narva line. Determined more than ever to crush the German defences Russian forces undertook a heavy assault in the Lilenbach area. The area was defended by men of the *Nederland's* 49.*SS-Freiwilligen*-Panzergrenadier-Regiment *de Ruyter*, commanded by *SS-Obersturmbannführer* Hans Collani, a Finnish veteran of the *Wiking* Division. Following a huge artillery duel between the *Nederland* and the Red Army attackers, the assuult disintegrated into fierce hand to hand fighting. After several hours of ferocious combat, the Russians withdrew with huge losses. *De Ruyter* had held the line, and the Soviets decided to shift the focus of their attack elsewhere.

Over the next weeks that followed, *Nederland* was subjected to almost constant artillery and aerial bombardments. On the night of 6/7 March, the Red Air Force made a huge bombing raid on Narva, flattening the city. This was followed by a sustained artillery attack with hundreds of artillery pieces. The *Nederland's* 48. *SS-Freiwilligen-*Panzergrenadier-Regiment *General Seyffardt,* commanded by *SS-Standartenführer* Wolfgang Jörchel, positioned to the south of *Danmark,* was attacked and forced from their positions. What followed was a ferocious counterattack with *SS* troops fighting in hand-to-hand combat.

All along the German defensive line fierce fighting continued throughout March and April, with the Russians obtaining little ground against the tenacious German defenders. During this period the Red Army increased their intensity of the bombardments. On 7 March, massed Russian air attacks attempted to pulverise the German defensive positions, which lasted for some twelve hours. This was followed by a large systematic artillery bombardment. However, by this stage the civilian population had already been evacuated from Narva, leaving the *Waffen-SS* defenders to dig deeper into the rubble-strewn streets of the city.

The main thrust of the Soviet attack was then moved against positions at Lilienbach, which was held by the Dutch volunteer regiment *De Ruiter.* Once again the *SS* held firm and fought to the last drop of blood. However, with huge losses in men and equipment, it was soon became apparent that they would no longer be able to hold their position for any appreciable length of time.

On 23 March, Hitler declared Narva a fortress and ordered the city to be held at all costs. But with ammunition running low and casualties rising, the defence of Narva seemed an impossible task. However, by early April the Germans were reprieved from the clutches of the Red Army as the spring thaw arrived, bringing the end to large-scale attacks. During April and May the front stagnated and allowed both sides to rest and regroup. By the end of May, as the ground began to dry, the Russians were planning for an all out attack against the town of Dolgaja Niva, held by the *Nordland's Danmark* regiment.

On 7 June, the stillness of the front was suddenly broken by the sound of hundreds of Soviet guns opening up all across the seven mile Narva front. The entire Thirteenth Air Army of the Red Air Force took to the skies against minimal *Luftwaffe* opposition. A massive combined air and ground attack was then unleashed against *Nordland's* positions, and over the next four days the *SS* desperately tried to hold their shattered defences against wave upon wave of strong infantry attacks. Despite futile attempts to hold back the Russian drive, by 12 June they had managed to break through the Danish lines and occupy the strongpoint known as *Post Sunshine.* Only scattered forces now blocked the Russian route to the bridges over the Narva River. One of these forces was the remnant of 7. *Kompanie Danmark,* commanded by *SS-Scharführer* Egon Christofferson. Although heavily outnumbered, Christofferson was not deterred by the strength of his opponent and quickly ordered his small force forward to meet the advancing Russians. For the next few hours both sides fought a series of savage close-quarter battles, before Christofferson's men finally recaptured *Post Sunshine,* and restored the line. Christofferson was awarded the Knight's Cross for his actions. Though the fighting continued for another two weeks, the Red Army made no progress against the remnants of *Danmark.*

In spite of the resilience displayed by the Germans at Narva, by mid-June the German bridgehead on the east bank, opposite the city, had been greatly reduced and its position was becoming more precarious with each day. As a consequence it was decided to finally pull back to a new defensive position further west, to the so-called Tannenberg Line or *Tannenbergstellung,* located on a series of hills to the west of Narva.

All along the Narva front both *Waffen-SS* and *Wehrmacht* soldiers fought shoulder-to-shoulder trying to stem the enemy onslaught. In spite of Hitler's orders to stand or die, a general withdrawal was made to the Tannenberg Line. As Steiner's *Korps* retreated the *Nederland* was tasked with covering the withdrawal, with the *General Seyyfardt* regiment and the artillery battalion to be the last units to withdraw across the battered Narva bridge. The regiment itself soon became pinned down in bitter fighting and attacked by both air and ground forces. Slowly and systematically the regiment was bled white and as the last few remnants of the force tried to escape the slaughter, they too were annihilated.

Elsewhere on the front the situation had also deteriorated. A massive Soviet push from the north had finally forced the 20. *Waffengrenadier*-Division *der SS* back over the River Narva. Reluctantly these Estonian volunteers were compelled to withdraw westwards, contesting every foot of ground as they retreated across into their homeland. The soldiers had experienced Soviet occupation before, they had no wish to repeat it, and so they fought on to the death.

The battle of Narva was finally over. While the Russians claimed victory, the Germans had in fact delayed the enemy advance for a number of months and inflicted terrible damage on their forces. Although the first half of 1944 had been a period of disasters for the German armies on the Eastern Front, Hitler had good reason to be pleased with the performance of his *Waffen-SS* divisions. They had shown their courage in the face of overwhelming strength and stood firm against almost impossible odds. Narva was one battle that stood as an example where the *SS* made sacrifice after sacrifice, often holding the line to allow other units to escape. Few other units could engender such confidence from their *Führer*, but the *Waffen-SS* were not supermen, and a time would come when they would finally be unable to stave off ultimate defeat.

By the summer of 1944 the *Waffen-SS* were fully aware that the Red Army had only been delayed, not halted. As both the southern and northern fronts withdrew and tried their best efforts to stabilise their precarious defences against a growing enemy force, news had reached them that the Allies had landed in Western Europe. Once again it was the *Waffen-SS* divisions that Hitler looked upon to save the desperate situation.

Ski troops of the 6.*SS*.Gebirgs-Division *Nord* serving in Finnish Karelia in February 1944. The division consisted of two regiments plus an independent battalion of *SS Gebirgsjäger*, three mountain artillery battalions and various

A signals operator of the Gebirgs *Nord* division in February 1944. The division remained in Finland until September 1944 and took part in the retreat through Lapland into Norway. In late 1944 it was withdrawn from Norway and shipped to Denmark, from where it joined German forces on the Western Front.

SS soldiers of the *Polizei-Division* use an old wooden hut as a temporary shelter during it withdrawal in early 1944.

SS troops are preparing to move out of the Slantsy region on the Northern Front in early 1944. Supplies are being loaded on a boat, which was the quickest method of transporting equipement, instead of using the roads through the surrounding forests to the city of Narva.

A MG 42 machine gun crew from an unidentified *SS* foreign volunteer unit near Leningrad in early 1944. Around the besieged city of Leningrad, *SS* volunteer units were deployed to prevent a breakthrough. The main *SS* forces in this sector consisted of the *Nordland, Nederland,* and the 15. and 19. *Waffengrenadier* Divisions from Latvia plus the Flemish Langemarck Brigade.

A *SS* gun crew during winter operations in northern Russia in early 1944. Most wear the reversible, insulated winter suit and are armed with the Kar 98K bolt-action rifle.

A *SS* mortar crew in action. The mortar was used extensively by the *Waffen-SS*, as it was with all German formations. It was light, easy to carry, and gave the soldier his own portable light artillery support. But it required training to use; even experienced mortar crews could take several projectiles to achieve one successful hit on a target.

A *SS* Ski trooper of the *Nord* division in action in early 1944. The soldier is armed with a white snow-camouflaged Kar 98K bolt-action rifle and blends well in the snow with his standard two-piece snowsuit and field cap.

SS ski troopers utilise a sled to move a wounded comrade across the snow. In spite of the terrors and casualties of the Russian winter of early 1944, the *Waffen-SS* performance did not go unnoticed. Although fighting against overwhelming superiority they had stubbornly clung onto every foot of terrain with vigour and determination.

Russian troops surrendered to a *SS* soldier armed with an MG 42 machine gun. Even though the *SS* were becoming hard pressed by 1944, they constantly ran a gauntlet against heavy enemy fire, rushing from one position to another, filling gaps wrenched open by the Soviet onslaught.

SS volunteers on the Northern Front near Leningrad in early 1944. All across the Leningrad Front the soldiers were often fighting through bitterly cold weather and holding on like grim death, knowing that anything less would mean that their homeland would soon be overrun by a nation that hated them.

SS volunteers near the Leningrad Front in early 1944. The troops take a much-needed rest and sit around open fire.

SS volunteers of the *Nederland* division wearing the familiar old-style two-piece winter camouflage suits on the defence lines at Narva in early 1944. By the end of January the Red Army had reached the defence lines at Narva, which ran from Narva itself, south along the banks of the River Narva, to the shores of Lake Peipus and down to Polotsk, northwest of Vitebsk.

SS volunteers of the *Nederland* division along a sector of the Narva defence lines in early February 1944. By the evidence of the spent ammunition boxes there appears to have been some heavy localised action against Russian forces.

Volunteers from the 19.*SS.Waffengrenadier-*Division from Latvia during its retreat from the Leningrad Front in early 1944. Although these troops were not regarded as `first rate`, they fought well and put up a series of staunch defensive actions. The knocked out Russian T-34 tank is evidence of their determination on the battlefield.

A SS volunteer soldier wearing an old-type camouflage smock armed with a captured Russian PPSh-41 machine gun.

Waffen-SS volunteers from *Heeresgruppe Nord* during spring operations in April 1944. The troops are moving forward into action armed with two antiquated 7.5cm Infantry Gun 18s. All of the soldiers appear to be wearing the standard old-style *SS* camouflage smocks.

A *SS-Untersturmführer* decorates a *SS-Sturmmann* for gallantry during fighting on the Eastern Front in the spring of 1944.

Two commanding officers are photographed following a military parade in Russia on the Northern Front in March 1944. The officer on the right holds the rank of an *SS-Untersturmführer*.

A group of artillery troops of the *SS-Polizei* division in March 1944. The majority of the soldiers are wearing the *SS* fur-lined anoraks. One of the men is wearing the reversible snow camouflage jacket's white side.

A soldier of the *SS-Polizei* division in a defensive position in northern Russia in March 1944. The soldier is wearing the standard field cap and shapeless single cotton winter camouflage garment. Being loose fitting, it could be easily worn over the uniform and equipment.

A *SS* field kitchen has been set up on the edge of a forest. To the left is a captured Russian mobile cooking cauldron. Altogether this field kitchen could produce some 29-gallons of soup or stew, as well as brew some 16-gallons of coffee.

A group of *SS* troops prepare to go out on a local patrol. All the soldiers have been issued with the *Waffen-SS* insulated winter coat and mittens, but not the matching trousers or insulated boots.

An *SS* crew pose for the camera beside their 10.5cm howitzer in March 1944. This position seems temporary as no real camouflage has been utilised to conceal the gun, other than a single piece of tarpaulin.

On the Russian Northern Front *SS* volunteers in the spring of 1944 prepare to use their howitzers against enemy targets. Wicker cases protecting the shells can be seen laid out ready to be primed.

Soldiers belonging to a *SS-Polizei* artillery unit are seen here with one of their horses exhausted by the constant marching and pulling of heavy guns. Tens of thousands of horses died as a result of fatigue on the Eastern Front, especially during the winter periods.

A *Waffen-SS* 10.5cm howitzer battery in March 1944. Batteries were typically positioned like this a number of times a day to keep pace with the advancing infantry and to avoid being targeted by the enemy.

A *SS* flak crew stand by their whitewashed 8.8cm Flak 18, which has been positioned beside a Russian log cabin in the winter of 1944.

PART III

Combat Deployment in the West 1944–45

6. Normandy Campaign

On the eve of the Allied invasion of France, four of the ten German armoured divisions in France and Belgium were *Waffen-SS*. They consisted of the 1.*SS*.Panzer-Division *Leibstandarte Adolf Hitler*, 2.*SS*.Panzer-Division *Das Reich*, 12.*SS*.Panzer-Division *Hitlerjugend*, and the 17.*SS*.Panzergrenadier-Division *Götz von Berlichingen*. Even by this late period German intelligence could not confirm with any degree of accuracy where the main Allied invasion would take place. As a consequence the bulk of the *Waffen-SS* divisions were not located in the Normandy sector under the command of the 7.*Armee*. The *Leibstandarte* was lying in the area of Bruges in Belgium, where it had been resting since the spring of 1944 and had become part of the High Command strategic reserve and, therefore under Hitler's direct control. *Das Reich* was still in the Toulouse area, where the level of partisan operations had increased. The new *Hitlerjugend* division had been transported by rail from Belgium and was moved close to its expected area of action between the lower Seine and Orne rivers, whilst the *Götz von Berlichingen* division was stationed in Thouars in France.

The *Hitlerjugend* division was the nearest of all the four *Waffen-SS* divisions to the actual Allied landing point. On paper the division had over 20,000 soldiers deployed for action in Normandy. Although it was short of a number of armoured vehicles, the troops were well equipped and armed. After nine months of intensive combat training their spirits were high and they were looking at the coming action with confidence. *Sturmmann* Jochen Leykauff scribbled in his diary just before the enemy unleashed the greatest amphibious attack in military history:

> Everyone was waiting in great anticipation for the Allied landings. We were all looking forward to our first action. The Allies planned to destroy the so-called 'baby milk division', as they labelled us, but we were not frightened of them. Sometimes we got so excited at the prospects of fighting, we got big-headed. Although we knew our enemy were superior in numbers, we all trusted our commanders who had become hardened in battle. We had known them since our training first began and we had enjoyed seeing them in the mud and firing live ammunition with steel helmets and machine guns. What really frightened us about the coming invasion were the bomber squadrons, which constantly droned above us dropping tons of bombs.[1]

Just hours before the Allied landings begun the 12.*SS*.Panzer-Division headquarters were informed that enemy paratroopers had jumped behind the coastal sector in Normandy. This, it was predicted, was the prelude to the main attack. A couple of hours later all units of the *Hitlerjugend* were made ready and prepared in their alarm positions. Ninety minutes before the Allied landings begun the *OKW* (*Oberkommando der Wehrmacht*) assigned the 12.*SS* to *Heeresgruppe B*. And yet, despite measures, assessments and orders of the German high and supreme command offices on the growing developments of an Allied landing, the *Hitlerjugend* were not released for action. Even when the enemy landed at 06:30 hrs, *OKW* still forbade them from being released, but did approve its advance.

During the course of 6 June convoys of trucks and Panzers of the division navigated the congested narrow roadways of Normandy, moving first into the area around Lisieux and then southwest of the city of Caen. During its march, in particular from early afternoon, the *Hitlerjugend* were constantly strafed by fighters, which disrupted the cohesion of many of the marching columns. By the following morning on 7 June, exhausted from more than a day's constant marching, the bulk of the *Hitlerjugend* had moved into the area north of Caen. By this time reports had confirmed that the enemy had managed to break through some parts of the coastal defences and pushed his attack inland. By 09.00 hrs *Sturmbannführer* Kurt 'Panzer' Meyer, the commander of a *Kampfgruppe* comprising three battalions of infantry and a considerable number of Pz.Kpfw.IV tanks, had set up his forward command post in the

Ardennes abbey. An hour later the first Panzers of the division moved forward into their assembly areas followed by young *SS* grenadiers wearing their distinctive green, yellow and brown camouflage smocks. Hidden beneath straw and branches the Panzers trained their powerful 7.5cm gun barrels towards the advancing enemy. From their positions they could make out the stout, olive-green Sherman tanks moving slowly across the front of their *Kampfgruppe* towards the Caen-Bayeux road. Suddenly the Sherman's opened fire and the first Panzer erupted in smoke and flame. Others were also hit and set ablaze by Canadian anti-tank guns. From their hideouts and freshly dug trenches, the youths crashed into action, opening up a ferocious barrage of fire on British and Canadian positions. At times the fighting was at close quarters, the boys pitching grenades and pumping machine-gun fire into the enemy lines. Although the continuous attack from the air disrupted the grenadiers assault, the teenagers of the 12.*SS* fought on. In the nearby village of Malon, the boys were feverishly taking up positions, stalking the enemy tanks with their deadly *Panzerfaust*, and destroying several of them. In total the grenadiers knocked out twenty-eight enemy tanks at a loss of six of their own. Many of the Allied soldiers were shocked at seeing teenagers in *SS* uniforms. It was their first encounter with the *Hitlerjugend* generation. For months prior to the invasion of Normandy, the Allies had ridiculed the *Hitlerjugend* as the baby-division. But to the soldiers that fought against the 12.*SS*, this was far from a division of badly trained teenagers. It was an elite division that inspired fear and, at the same time, fought a battle that even inspired its enemies.

Over the next few days, as the battle of Normandy intensified, the *Hitlerjugend* came under even heavier attacks. But still this did not discourage the grenadiers from being driven from their bombed and blasted positions, for they had been given orders to hold the enemy at all costs and prevent them from penetrating their lines and breaking through to the ancient city of Caen.

During the evening of 9 June the Panzer-*Lehr*-Division moved into line alongside the 12.*SS* after driving miles to the front from Chartres. The following day the 21.Panzer-Division also moved up and helped the other two divisions form the principal shield around Caen, with a motley selection of other ad hoc units that had retreated from the coastal sector. For the next days and weeks that followed the *Hitlerjugend*, Panzer-*Lehr* division and the 21.Panzer carried on fighting superbly in and around the city of Caen, which was slowly being reduced to rubble. All day and night the fighting raged. Many soldiers were killed at point blank range, whilst others fighting in the hedgerows and ditches, fought to the death. Through the lanes and farm tracks that criss-crossed the Normandy countryside, rows of dead from both sides lay sprawled amid a mass of smashed and burnt out vehicles.

On 14 June the commander of the 12.*SS*, *Brigadeführer* Fritz Witt was killed at his divisional command post in Venoix, near Caen and was replaced by Kurt Meyer. At only 33 years old, with Iron Cross, First and Second Class and the Knight's Cross with Oak Leaves, Meyer was the youngest divisional commander in the German armed forces. Out on the battlefield he was a daredevil commander of unorthodox methods and fought his battles deep inside enemy lines. But despite his skill and courageous character the change of command in the 12.*SS* made no tactical difference. In fact, he took command of the division on the edge of disaster. Fighting for the defence of Caen had continued with massive losses, despite the preparation of new defences to prevent an enemy offensive on the city.

By the morning of 26 June, the British finally unleashed a large-scale attack on Caen code-named *Operation Epsom*. During the day's fighting at least 50 enemy tanks were knocked out by the Panzers and Pak guns alone. But the Panzergrenadiers took a heavy battering, and in some areas a number of battalions were totally wiped out along with their commanders. Over the next few days the Allies continued to strike out, smashing onto the 12.*SS* lines and causing massive damage to their positions. In the days leading up to July, the British, endeavouring to expand their bridgehead, became increasingly incensed at the conduct of the *Hitlerjugend* division, who fought so tenaciously when their cause was so clearly lost. This dogged determination had managed to finally blunt the Epsom operation, which consequently prevented it from achieving the high plain south of Caen. But in spite of this success the division was badly depleted and its survivors exhausted. Most of the German forces around the city were in desperate need of being replenished.

On 5 July, news reached *Heeresgruppe B* that Hitler contemplated having the *Hitlerjugend* relieved. However, three days later the *SS* division were once again fighting another battle for Caen, codenamed by the Allies as *Operation Charnwood*. Once again Meyer's 'boys' were the core of the defence, and fought out the battle in the ruins around Caen with an aura that they were indestructible, even though their ranks had been decimated after weeks of continued defence. As the battle reached its peak, Hitler ordered the city to be held at all costs. But with no more reserves left and ammunition rapidly running out, Meyer ordered the withdrawal of the division and instructed them take up a new defensive position in the rear.

By 11 July the *Hitlerjugend* was relieved by the *Leibstandarte Adolf Hitler* division, which took command of two units that remained in action. For nearly a week the *Leibstandarte* battled in the Caen region in a desperate attempt to stem the advancing Allies. On 18 July the British launched their second offensive, *Operation Goodwood*. This was an advance by three armoured divisions with the main objective of capturing the high ground north of Caen, and weakening *Panzergruppe* West, so as to allow the American *Operation Cobra* to break out along the Cotentin Peninsula.

Operation Cobra begun with a massive combined aerial and ground bombing attack that saw some of the *Leibstandarte* units suffering severe losses. However, this did not discourage the *SS* soldiers, and still under the constant hammer blows of enemy artillery and anti-tank fire, the Panzers of *Leibstandarte* and the 21.Panzer-Division moved forward to counterattack, supported by grenadiers huddled behind the hulls for protection. For this counterattack the *SS* could only muster forty-six armoured fighting vehicles and some self-propelled guns, but these were formed into a powerful two-pronged assault. Within hours of the counter-attack the Germans had successfully flung back the British spearheads. The British lost more than 200 tanks, while between them the Germans lost 109 tanks – but the line had held.

The following day on 19 July the British attacked again, and at Bras in a fierce hand-to-hand battle annihilated a complete *Leibstandarte* grenadier battalion. On 20 July a Canadian Corps attacked the important Vassieres ridge and smashed through the 272.*Infanterie*-Division behind which the *Leibstandarte* was in reserve. *SS* grenadiers fought a desperate close quarter action, which saw both sides sustaining terrible casualties. Although later that day *Operation Goodwood* was called off, both the British and Canadians continued keeping seven of the remaining nine Panzer divisions occupied in the Caen sector.

Six divisions of the American First and Third Armies had meanwhile moved south on the western side of the Cherbourg peninsula. The only German armoured divisions in their path were the 2.SS.Panzer-Division *Das Reich*, and the 17.SS.Panzergrenadier-Division *Götz von Berlichingen*. The *Das Reich* division had journeyed from Toulouse in the south of France and had been seriously delayed reaching the Normandy sector by partisan activity and the constant aerial attacks. The convoys of the division had been unable to carry out daylight movement and had crawled northwards through the darkness. All the Panzer divisions that arrived in the Normandy sector were in such bad shape that they needed days to regroup before going into action. German wireless signals were continuously jammed with Panzer commanders requesting fuel, transportation, new routings and other important material needed to sustain their drive. *Das Reich* division was no exception. It arrived exhausted in the rear areas of the battlefront between 15 and 30 June, nearly three weeks behind schedule.

The division was not inserted into the Normandy campaign until 10 July, by which time it had already suffered heavy losses. Despite its severe mauling by Allied bombing, the division was far from beaten.

On 29 July the combined force of *Das Reich* and *Götz von Berlichingen* attacked American forces near St.Denis le Gast, but the attack was soon suppressed by overwhelming Allied numerical superiority. On the same day the British launched *Operation Bluecoat*, an assault in the direction of Vire on the boundary between American and British forces. During this critical period the *Heeresgruppe* quickly brought all available Panzer units from the south of Caen to deal with the enemy threat. On the 2 August following heavy fighting, Vire was entered by the British, but was quickly recaptured by two *SS* Panzer divisions the next day.

All over the Normandy sector the *Waffen-SS* divisions continued desperately to try and keep the Allies in check. The Norman countryside had created conditions that favoured the *SS* grenadiers. Clusters of trees, tall hedges, ditches, and lack of roads frustrated the Allied armoured units seeking to destroy enemy tanks in open areas. Aided by this terrain the *SS* were able to defend positions longer than the Allies had expected were possible, and as a result incurred huge casualties. Frequently the Allies watched their irrepressible foe come under a furious crescendo of mortar and shellfire, and still they held their ground to the grim death. However, the savage Allied air attacks and naval bombardments gradually began to grind down the German defences. Movement was almost impossible by daylight, and any vehicles that travelled during the day were attacked and destroyed.

By the end of the first week of August both the *Wehrmacht* and *Waffen-SS* divisions were fighting for survival. Corps and divisions remained in action on paper, but were becoming a small collection of units, shrinking down to battalion size. A catastrophe now threatened the whole area as the Americans began to break out and the Normandy campaign became mobile. To save the German forces in Normandy from being completely encircled and destroyed a series of rapid withdrawals were undertaken through the Falaise-Argentan gap. On 16 August German forces continued retreating and crossed the River Orne. The *Hitlerjugend* division desperately fought to keep the gap open. The bulk of the German armour, however, that had become trapped inside the pocket at Falaise fought a desperate battle to escape the impending slaughter. By 21 August, the terrible fighting in what became famously known as the battle of the Falaise Pocket drew to a catastrophic conclusion. The *Waffen-SS* had been dealt a heavy blow.

The Normandy campaign had been very costly for the *Waffen-SS*, with many of its elite units being annihilated. The *Leibstandarte* had suffered almost total destruction. *Das Reich* had some 450 men and 15 tanks remaining; the *Hohenstaufen* had 460 men and some 25 tanks that had survived the slaughter. The 10.SS.Panzer-Division *Frundsberg* lost all of its tanks and artillery, whilst the *Hitlerjugend* had only 300 men remaining and no artillery.

Following the complete German defeat in France, remnants of its forces withdrew for rest and refitting. The *Leibstandarte* was withdrawn to Aachen; *Das Reich* limped back to the Schnee Eifel area, the *Hitlerjugend* was pulled out and sent back east of Maas in Belgium and *Götz von Berlichingen* was moved to Metz. The *Hohenstaufen* and *Frundsberg* divisions were withdrawn to lick their wounds in a quite backwater in Holland. It was a town called Arnhem.

In spite of the almost total destruction of the *Waffen-SS*, the campaign in the West had proved like the battles had done so much in the East, that they could only delay the enemy, not defeat them.

Within months of the Normandy campaign the *Waffen-SS* would once again be ready and refitted for action. However, it was not to be another delaying action. This time the *SS* troops were to go over to the attack in a bold and daring offensive through the Ardennes region. This was to be known as the *Führer's* last gamble in the West.

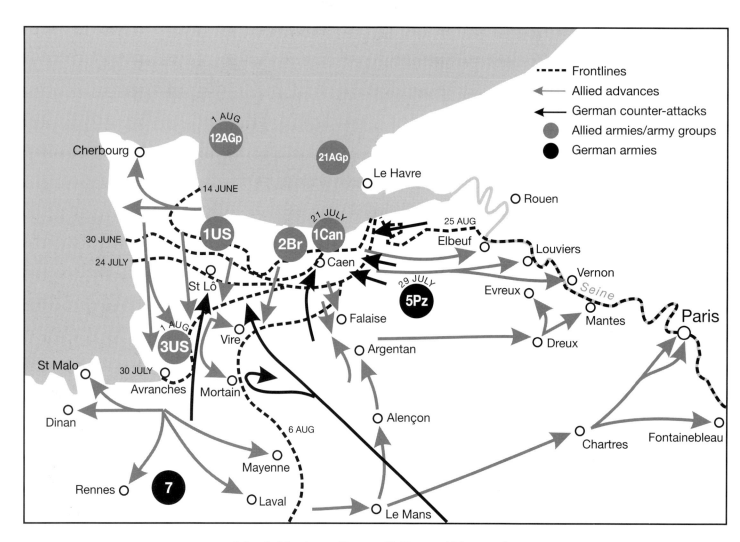

Map 3: Northwest Europe, D-Day and Normandy

Two *SS* soldiers inside a 166 Volkswagen amphibious reconnaissance vehicle during the early summer of 1944.

A Tiger tank crew are loading shells through the rear stowage hatch of their vehicle in May 1944. It was in northern France that the *Waffen-SS* Tiger I units made valuable contributions to the German defence in the West during the summer of 1944.

A *SS* Pz.Kpfw.IV tank commander armed with an MP38/40 sub machine gun poses for the camera prior to his departure to the battlefront during the Normandy landings in June 1944. The Pz.Kpfw.IV performed well in defensive operations against the Allies in Normandy and both the *Leibstandarte* and its sister division the 12.*SS Hitlerjugend* were strengthened with a number of these tanks to repel the invaders.

Leibstandarte troops relax in a field near Bruges in Belgium in early June 1944. By the time the Allied invasion of Northern France was unleashed, the *Leibstandarte* was not called into action immediately, as it was still part of the Armed Forces High Command's strategic reserve.

A *Leibstandarte* Sd.Kfz.251. halftrack with a 10.5cm field gun on tow stationary in a field near Bruges in Belgium. It was not until 17 June 1944, 11 days after the invasion, that this elite *Waffen-SS* division would finally be committed to combat to the Normandy sector around Caen.

SS troops gather for a last photograph before being committed to the Normandy sector to repel the Allied landings.

A *Leibstandarte* flak unit towing a 2cm flak gun during the Division's march to the Normandy sector in June 1944.

A *SS* soldier with camouflaged scissor binoculars jots down notes of the location and probable strength of Allied forces south of Caen in June 1944.

Leibstandarte troops on the rear of an infantry truck have halted in a field prior to their deployment into the city of Caen, where their sister division the *Hitlerjugend* was already fighting fiercely in a bloody battle of attrition.

SS troops are hiding in a trench during a heavy Allied bombing raid on their sector during the early days of the Normandy campaign. Allied bombing was a constant hindrance to the movement of German troops in Northern France and resulted in terrible casualties. In some sectors of the front more than three-quarters of *SS* strength was totally annihilated as a consequence of systematic aerial attacks.

SS armour of the *Götz von Berlichingen* division. This *SS* Panzergrenadier division had been formed in November 1943 and was working up in the area around Tours/Angers. It was brought into the line at Normandy within a week of the initial landings.

On the move, a column of *Leibstandarte* vehicles rumbles along a road bound for the battlefront south of Caen in June 1944.

SS mechanics belonging to a field maintenance company replace the Maybach HL230 P45 V12 engine of a Tiger I during the Normandy campaign. The independent Tiger battalions owed much of their success to their well-equipped maintenance companies, which kept the vehicles in fighting condition.

A well-camouflaged Panther tank belonging to the *Hitlerjugend* division. It was in desperate defensive fighting in Normandy that the Panther tanks proved their worth. The Panthers were often deployed in ambush positions in woods, where they scored sizable successes against unsuspected Allied forces.

69

A *SS Kampfgruppe* belonging to the famous *Hitlerjugend* division take cover during a lull in the fighting around Caen in June 1944. This *Kampfgruppe* was under the command of *SS-Standartenführer* Kurt `Panzer` Meyer. It comprised three battalions of infantry and a considerable number of Pz.Kpfw.IV tanks from the Division's Panzer regiment.

Motorcycle combinations and Pz.Kpfw.IV tanks have halted in a field in late June 1944. These late variant Panzers with intact armoured side skirts are part of the *Das Reich* division. The division was initially stationed in southern France near Toulouse, but was ordered north to the Normandy Sector. It did not reach the area until 10 July, where it was moved into the line near Periers.

A *Das Reich* flak crew preparing for action following their long bloody march from Toulouse.

A 2cm Flakvierling 38 quadruple-barrelled self-propelled anti-aircraft gun mounted on the back of a Sd.Kfz.7 halftrack during operations in the Caen area in July 1944.

7. 'Watch on the Rhine'

By the summer of 1944 the *Waffen-SS*, along with its *Wehrmacht* counterpart, had come close to being completely annihilated on the Western Front. However, within months it had miraculously undergone recovery. Many of the divisions that had been battered in Normandy and then smashed to pieces in the Falaise Pocket and the subsequent retreat across France, were now rebuilt. New divisions had been raised or brought in for refitting in Germany or the Eastern Front. On paper it seemed that there was still hope, but in reality many German units still seriously lacked transport and the appropriate numbers of officers and non-commissioned officers. A great number of units had barely half their proper amount of the major items of equipment.

But in spite of the shortages, in September 1944, just two months following the Normandy campaign Hitler had decided to launch a great winter counter-attack in the West. The attack he envisaged would be through the Ardennes – the scene of his great 1940 victory –with the aim of capturing the town of Antwerp. 'Fog, night, and snow', would be on his side. With Antwerp in German hands, he predicted the British and Americans would have no port from which to escape, but this time the enemy would not be allowed to escape.

The proposal at first seemed too adventurous. The fact that almost a million German soldiers had been lost since the Allied invasion of France would never have led commanders to conceive that a nation so close to death could perform a dazzling display of military ingenuity. And, yet within three months of drafting the plan thousands of troops and armour were moved into the Ardennes and prepared to unleash an offensive that would totally surprise the Allies.

Here in the Ardennes a substantial number of divisions were assigned to the area, including four crack *Waffen-SS* units; 1.*SS. Leibstandarte Adolf Hitler*, 2.*SS.Das Reich*, 9.*SS.Hohenstaufen*, and 12.*SS.Hitlerjugend*. These SS divisions were larger than the regular *Wehrmacht* Panzer divisions, and totalled a ground strength between 16,000 and 20,000 soldiers, with three-battalion Panzergrenadier regiments, a slightly larger artillery regiment that included a battalion of Nebelwerfers and a *Sturmgeschütz Abteilung* with twenty or thirty assault guns. The *SS* also had a higher allotment of motor vehicles. However, they were still below their assigned strength for officers and non-commissioned officers, mostly because of the terrible losses sustained in Normandy.

The equipment used by the *SS* armoured formations in the Ardennes was generally excellent, although by this late period of the war it was still in short supply. The forces committed to the battle zone contained a number of independent self-propelled anti-tank and heavy tank battalions and several assault gun brigades, which were battalion size formations. There were four *schwere Panzerjäger* battalions, nominally equipped with a mix of *Jagdpanthers*, *Panzerjäger* IVs, and *Sturmgeschütz* IIIs. The *schwere* Panzer battalions contained the famous Tiger heavy tanks. Three of these units were committed in the Ardennes and the *501.SS* was attached to the *Leibstandarte*. The lead element of the *501.SS Schwere Panzer Abteilung* was commanded by the veteran armoured ace *Obersturmbannführer* Joachim Peiper, commander of the 1.*SS.Panzer-Regiment*.

For the attack in the Ardennes, the *Waffen-SS* was assigned for action with the *6.Panzer-Armee*, which was to deliver the decisive blow. It was commanded by *Oberstgruppenführer* Josef Sepp Dietrich, who had fought brilliantly on the Eastern Front and commanded the *I.SS.Panzer-Korps*, comprising of the 1. and 12.*SS*.Panzer divisions in the Normandy Campaign. The *6.Panzer-Armee* contained all the four *SS*.Panzer divisions and was given the task of tearing huge holes in the American lines between the Losheim Gap and Monschau.

To the south of the *6.Panzer.Armee's* sector lay General der *Panzertruppen* Hasso von Manteuffel's *5.Panzer.Armee* and General Erich Brandenberger's *7.Armee*, which was the southernmost of the three armies committed to the offensive. Altogether the five Panzer and Panzergrenadier divisions and thirteen infantry-type divisions, consisting of *Fallschirmjäger* and *Volksgrenadier* troops were to be unleashed through the Belgium and Luxembourg countryside. The codename for this historic offensive was *Wacht am Rhein* (Watch on the Rhine), and it was planned to begin on the early morning of 16 December 1944.

Waffen-SS Order Of Battle, Ardennes 15 December 1944

I.SS.Panzer-Korps

277.Volksgrenadier-Division
989.Grenadier-Regiment
990.Grenadier-Regiment

991.Grenadier-Regiment
277.Panzerjäger–Battalion
277.Artillery Regiment
277.Engineer Battalion
9.SS.Panzer-Artillery-Regiment (assigned)

1st SS Panzer-Division

1.SS.Panzergrenadier-Regiment
2.SS.Panzergrenadier-Regiment
1.SS.Panzer-Regiment
501.SS.Heavy-Panzer-Battalion
1.SS.Panzer-Artillery-Regiment
1.SS.Panzer-Engineer-Battalion
1.SS.Panzerjäger-Battalion
84.Flak-Battalion (assigned)
Reserve
1.SS.Flak-Battalion
1.SS.Panzer-Engineer-Battalion
12.Nebelwerfer-Regiment (assigned)
9.Volkswerfer-Brigade (assigned)

12.SS.Panzer-Division Hitlerjugend

25.SS.Panzergrenadier-Regiment
26.SS.Panzergrenadier-Regiment
12.SS.Panzer-Artillery-Regiment
12.SS.Flak-Battalion
12.SS.Panzer-Engineer-Battalion
12.SS.Panzer-Regiment
12.SS.Nebelwerfer-Battalion
14.Nebelwerfer-Regiment (assigned)
9.Volksgrenadier-Brigade (assigned)

Supporting I.SS.Panzer-Korps

3.Fallschirmjäger-Division

5. Fallschirmjäger-Regiment
8.Fallschirmjäger-Regiment
9.Fallschirmjäger-Regiment
3.Fallschirmjäger-Panzerjäger-Battalion
3.Fallschirmjäger-Artillery Regiment
3.Fallschirmjäger-Engineer Battalion
3.Fallschirmjäger-Heavy Mortar Battalion

4.Volkswerfer-Brigade

1098.Artillery Battery
1123.Artillery Battery
388.Volks-Artillery-Korps
402.Volks-Artillery Battalion
501.SS.Heavy Artillery Battalion
502.SS.Heavy Artillery Battalion
3.Flak-Assault-Regiment

(Army reserve) II.SS.Panzer-Korps

2.SS.Panzer-Division
9.SS.Panzer-Division
(generic organisation of both above divisions similar to 1st SS Panzer Division).

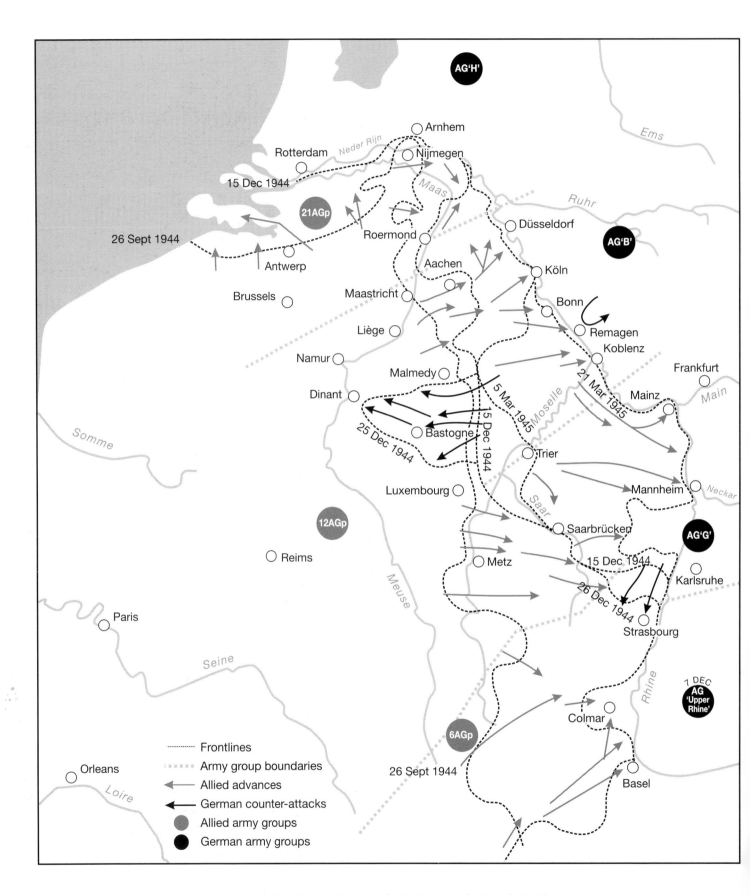

Map 4: Northwest Europe, the Drive into the Reich 1944

By mid-December, all German forces were in place and ready to unleash the largest offensive since Kursk two years before. All along the German front from Monschau in the north to Echternach on the Luxembourg border, the cold dawn of 16 December was broken by shouts of German gunnery officers giving the order for their men to begin a massive artillery barrage. Across the rolling hills, dense pine forests, deeply cut ravines and narrow roads the Ardennes erupted in a wall of flame and smoke. Two thousand light, medium, and heavy guns, howitzers and *Nebelwerfers* poured fire and destruction onto enemy positions. Shell after shell thundered into American strong points. Some American soldiers fearing complete annihilation scrambled from their sleeping bags and threw themselves into shelters and foxholes.

In the north *6.Panzer-Armee* inflicted the heaviest barrage of fire. At least 657 guns and howitzers of various calibre and 340 *Nebelwerfers* were directed on American positions between Hofen and Losheim Gap. For almost an hour without interruption, shells screamed over the heads of the waiting German infantry. Abruptly the bombardment ended, leaving a stunned silence for a few moments. Then beneath the pines and camouflage netting, thousands of German soldiers began their 'historic offensive'.

The *Volksgrenadiers*, many going into battle for the first time, were excited at the thought of fighting an offensive that their *Führer* had said would drive the invaders from their homeland and win them the greatest victory since Dunkirk. The *Volksgrenadiers* were closely followed by the tanks and elite *Waffen-SS* Panzer divisions. The spearhead of the *6.Panzer-Armee* was to be formed by *I.SS.Panzer-Korps*, which had been tasked with smashing through American lines between Hollerath and Krewinkel and driving through to Liege-Huy sector with the *Hitlerjugend* on the right flank and the *Leibstandarte* on the left. The *I.SS.Panzer-Korps* was given a particular powerful *Kampfgruppe*, which was led by *SS. Obersturmbannführer* Joachim Peiper.

Kampfgruppe Peiper's progress had proven difficult and his powerful Tigers were often confined to the narrow, twisting roads because the terrain was largely unsuitable for cross-country movement. Peiper was a ruthless tank commander and had commanded a tank battalion in Russia, which had become known as the *Blowtorch battalion* because allegedly it burned to the ground two villages, killing all the inhabitants. This same ruthlessness was also to mark *Kampfgruppe Peiper's* drive across the Ardennes. In the town of Honsfeld Peiper's *SS* grenadiers surprised American soldiers, and as they fled in panic and confusion they were shot, whilst a number of them surrendered. It was here that Peiper's men began their trail of massacres by murdering 19 American soldiers who had capitulated.

Within the first twenty-four hours of the offensive Peiper's *Kampfgruppe* continued to exploit the American defences using every means at its disposal to annihilate all enemy resistance. In Manderfeld on 17 December, American soldiers were completely taken by surprise by the appearance of *SS* tanks moving through the town, and surrendered after offering little resistance. By this time Peiper had already reported that he was running low on fuel and was compelled to divert his tanks towards Bullingen and capture an American fuel dump there. This consequently allowed his force time to replenish their thirsty Tigers, before moving forward on to capture Schoppen, Ondenval and Thirimont. The *Kampfgruppe* then advanced on Ligneuville, where it met fierce resistance from American troops supported by Sherman tanks. Following its successful capture Peiper set up a command post in the town whilst the rest of his *Kampfgruppe* moved on towards Trois Ponts and Beaumont. At Stavelot the *Kampfgruppe* met strong enemy resistance and were compelled to withdraw for the night and wait for the arrival of Peiper the following morning, before resuming the attack. The following day under the command of Peiper the *SS* once again attacked and captured the bridge at Stavelot intact, and then moved into the town clearing out all enemy resistance. The *Kampfgruppe* then pressed on towards Trois Ponts, but was forced to divert its forces because the Americans had succeeded in blowing the bridge over the Ambleve.

By 19 December, Peiper had reached Stoumont, where a vicious two-hour battle raged with Americans trying at all costs to hold the town. When the town could no longer be held the Americans quickly retreated, but Peiper's tanks pursued them for a few miles out of the town, before eight of their own tanks were brought to a flaming halt at an American road block.

In spite of the successful German advance through the Ardennes, the Allies were now beginning to recover from the initial surprise and resistance was stiffening day by day. By 22 December the Americans began stemming the German drive. Coupled with the lack of fuel and the constant congestions on the narrow roads many German units were brought to a standstill. The fuel shortages were so bad that on 23 December Peiper's *Kampfgruppe* destroyed their vehicles, and his remaining 1,000 men set out on foot for the German lines. The remnants of the *Kampfgruppe* then linked up with the *Leibstandarte* just before dawn on Christmas day.

Along the entire front German soldiers were becoming increasingly exhausted. Even the *Waffen-SS* had become worn down. For days and night, in the wet and cold, they had pushed westwards towards a promised victory. Nourished by their early success and apparent lack of resistance, their forces began to wither as shortages of rations, lack of sleep, and the constant shelling and bombing from aerial attacks drained their energy. With the *SS* armoured spearheads bedevilled by broken lines of communication and lack of fuel, the Ardennes offensive begun to ground to a halt less than two weeks after it was unleashed.

In a drastic attempt to assist the failing drive to the Meuse River, additional troops were thrown in to launch a new offensive in Alsace, where the Americans had drained their forces in order to send reinforcements north into the Ardennes. The code-name was *Nordwind*, and it was launched in earnest on New Year's Day with eight divisions spearheaded by an *SS Korps* consisting of the 17.*SS*.Panzergrenadier-Division *Götz von Berlichingen* and the 36.Volksgrenadier-Division. At first the offensive went relatively well, but heavy resistances soon forced the Germans back. The subsequent commitment of the 10.*SS*.Panzer-Division *Frundsberg* and the 6.*SS*.Gebirgs-Division *Nord* failed to alter the situation in the area.

In the Ardennes, the *Leibstandarte, Hohenstaufen* and *Hitlerjugend* divisions were heavily embroiled in fierce fighting around the town of Bastogne. The German capture of the town was not a symbolic one. It was essential to the successful development of their offensive through Belgium. Around the smouldering town the *Waffen-SS* fought with great energy and determination. Both sides incurred huge losses, but still the Americans were resolute in defending the town and preventing the enemy from gaining entry.

During the first days of January 1945, the weather became even more appalling, with temperatures falling to around zero. Fighting through fog, sleet and deep snow caused discouragement and pessimism to spread on both sides, and even the crack *SS* divisions begun faltering. Around Bastogne the Germans were eventually forced on the defensive and driven back. Nearly 12,000 German troops were killed attempting to capture Bastogne and 900 Americans died defending it, with another 3,000 killed outside the perimeter. From the pulverising effects of ground and aerial attacks, the Germans had left behind 450 tanks and armoured vehicles.

The defeat outside Bastogne was yet another major blow to the German command and marked the turning point of the offensive. All across their battered front fighting had begun to get harder and resistance was difficult to overcome. Troops constantly found themselves beating the enemy at terrible cost only to find a few miles on, fresh, well-armed American troops waiting for them.

With so many Allied troops being employed in the Ardennes, it slowly forced Hitler to realize how dangerous the war in the West had become. On 8 January, with more than 100,000 Germans casualties on the battlefield, the *Führer* grudgingly ordered the remnants of the forward units to fall back to a line running south from Dochamps, in the Samree-Baraque de Fraiture area, to Longchamps, five miles north of Bastogne. Even more significant were orders for the mighty elite *SS* Panzer divisions to go over to the defensive. The 6.*SS*.Panzer-Armee was withdrawn into reserve under Hitler's personal command and he also called back remnants of his foremost fighting machine – the *Leibstandarte* from the Bastogne area. Panzers coming off the assembly lines were diverted from the Ardennes back to the Eastern Front, and there were no more propaganda broadcasts in Germany about the 'historic offensive'.

By 24 January all four *Waffen-SS* divisions that were initially committed to the Ardennes campaign were withdrawn and ordered to Hungary in a drastic attempt to throw the Red Army back across the Danube and to relieve the capital, Budapest. As for the remaining forces in the Ardennes sector they were withdrawn and the remaining units were back over the Rhine by 10 February, preparing to fight the last battle of the *Reich*.

A *SS* MG 42 machine gunner opens fire across a field during the early stages of the Ardennes offensive in December 1944.

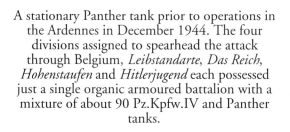

A stationary Panther tank prior to operations in the Ardennes in December 1944. The four divisions assigned to spearhead the attack through Belgium, *Leibstandarte, Das Reich, Hohenstaufen* and *Hitlerjugend* each possessed just a single organic armoured battalion with a mixture of about 90 Pz.Kpfw.IV and Panther tanks.

SS troops huddle in a trench prior to going into action during the opening phases of the Ardennes offensive.

A *SS* Nebelwerfer battalion launch their fearsome rockets against American positions during the morning of 15 December 1944. A Nebelwerfer proved lethal against enemy positions and could cause serious death and destruction.

A *SS* soldier with his Pak 40 gun during operations in the Ardennes in late December 1944. By this period of the offensive, as the Allies once again resumed heavy aerial attacks, the Germans were aware that success could no longer be achieved.

SS grenadiers during Operation *Nordwind* cross a river in the province of Alsace in early January 1944. Among the *Waffen-SS* units to take part were *Götz von Berlichingen* and the Gebirgs *Nord* division, which had recently been evacuated from the far north of the Eastern Front.

A *SS* grenadier digs a foxhole with his entrenching tool whilst one of his comrades moves forward along a frozen dirt road. By the end of 1944 the whole offensive in the Ardennes was now bogged down, as Allied numerical superiority and air power, combined with German supply problems, began to take their toll.

A *SS* flak crew belonging to *Götz von Berlichingen* during Operation *Nordwind*. Although initial success was achieved, the attack foundered within a few days. In spite of a number of further attacks by the *SS* to stabilise the deteriorating situation, no further gains were made in the area.

A *Waffen-SS* soldier photographs captured black American soldiers who were taken during the opening phase of the Ardennes offensive. The dejected column of GI`s pass a stationary 166 Volkswagen amphibious reconnaissance vehicle.

Here an unidentified *SS* unit is east of the Rhine in March 1945. By 10 February 1945, the last German units were back over the Rhine. All that was left for the *Wehrmacht* and *Waffen-SS* was to fight a dogged, but hopeless, rearguard action, as the Americans, Canadians, French and British pushed through into Germany.

A StuG.III. Ausf.G moves forward to prepare for the final defence of Germany in March 1945. The StuG still retains its summer camouflage scheme and one of its armoured side skirts is missing, indicating that it's been lost whilst participating in fighting.

One of the most popular forms of getting from one part of the front to another was by hitching a lift onboard a tank. Here in this photograph *SS* grenadiers ride onboard a column of StuG.III`s in February 1945.

A *SS* artillery unit have used extensive camouflage to conceal their weapons from enemy observation during the last battles fought in Germany in early April 1945.

A *SS* flak crew of the *Reichsführer-SS* division in northern Italy in early 1945. Although the *Waffen-SS* did not play a major role in operations in Italy, they nonetheless left an indelible mark on the Italian people with a series of savage reprisals against the population for suspected collusion with a number of partisan bands.

SS soldiers during a lull in the fighting share soup from a single mess tin. These soldiers belong to the *Reichsführer-SS* division, which by January 1945 was in position in the far north east of Italy. The division was soon assembled for a counterattack in the Lake Balaton area of the Eastern Front.

SS troops being transported to the front to fight out the last defensive battles in the West. The dusty conditions have compelled all of the soldiers to wear aviator goggles to protect their eyes.

A *SS* 35/36 Pak crew prepare to fire another projectile against the advancing enemy. The 35/36 Pak gun had become the first anti-tank gun to serve the *Waffen-SS*. Although the crews that used the weapon came to appreciate its tactical limitations, it still served frontline *SS* units until the end of the war, especially in volunteer divisions.

A whitewashed Pz.Kpfw.IV during winter operations in Germany in early March 1945. In spite of battlefield inferiority the *Waffen-SS* still continued to use the Pz.Kpfw.IV in significant defensive operations in the West, where they fought tenaciously until the very last days of the war.

The last battles in the West are being fought out. In this photograph two vehicles that still retain their winter camouflage scheme can be seen abandoned as *Waffen-SS* grenadiers unleash an attack against superior Allied forces in March 1945.

A *SS* tank crew take a brief respite during a lull in the fighting on the Western Front in early April 1945. The late variant Pz.Kpfw.IV has a full summer camouflage scheme. Note the spare track links that have been attached to the side of the vehicle for additional armoured protection.

SS troops press an inflatable boat into service during operations on the Western Front in the spring of 1945.

PART IV

Combat Deployment in the East
Autumn 1944-Spring 1945

8. Defending Poland

By June 1944, German strategy was faced with a full-fledged two-front war. More than fifty-three percent of the army was fighting in Russia, whilst the other forty-seven percent were in Western Europe trying to stem the Allied invasion along the Normandy coast. On the Eastern Front the German Army strength had reached a new low of some 2,242,649 against more than six million Russian troops. The best-equipped and most effective segment of the German force, the *Waffen-SS*, reached a strength of some 400,000 men. Of this total the bulk of the most elite *SS* combat formations were fighting in France. In the East the *SS* were distributed on the northern, central and southern fronts and were intended to act as the backbone of the German fighting machine. Many of its commanders were well aware of the seriousness of the military situation and looked ahead to the coming battles, knowing that that they were bound by orders which they could not successfully achieve. In front of them stood a huge enemy army whose strength was almost three times their own.

During the first week of June reports multiplied as news reached the various German commands that the Russians were preparing a new summer offensive on the central front. By the morning of 22 June 1944, the third anniversary of the invasion of Russia, the long awaited Soviet offensive was launched against *Heeresgruppe Mitte*. In total the First Baltic and Third Belorussian Fronts hurled more than 2.5 million troops, 4,000 tanks, 25,000 artillery pieces and mortars, and 5,300 aircraft to the northwest and southwest of Vitebsk. In opposition the Germans could only field 1,200,000 men, 9,500 guns and 900 tanks, with some 1,300 or so aircraft.

The Russian offensive was code-named *Operation Bagration*, and within twenty-fours hours of the attack Soviet forces had smashed through the lines of *Heeresgruppe Mitte*. In just seven days, the entire length of a 200-mile front stretching from Ostrov on the Lithuanian border and Kovel on the edge of the Pripet Marshes had been completely overrun. In just twelve days *Heeresgruppe Mitte* had lost 25 divisions. Of its original 165,000-man strength, *4.Armee* lost a staggering 130,000 soldiers. The *3.Panzer-Armee* lost 10 divisions. The *9.Armee*, however, held onto its pocket long enough for some 10,000 of its troops to escape the slaughter. In a drastic attempt to stabilise the crumbling lines the *Totenkopf* division had been rushed north to join the *4.Armee*, but became delayed in the chaos and carnage that befell *Heeresgruppe Mitte*. As the Germans pulled back, the Red Army continued its remorseless drive westwards, carving its way through towards the borders of East Prussia and Poland.

Over the next few weeks *Heeresgruppe Mitte* drifted westwards towards Kaunas, the Neman River, and Bialystok. The Red Army forces were moving faster than the Germans could deploy their meagre troops, even to attempt a stand. But the Russians having covered more than 200 miles without pause had temporarily outstripped their supplies and as a consequence slowed their advance to a crawl. The Germans, consequently, took advantage of the situation and tried their best to regroup and plug sectors in the front that had been punched through by the enemy. What was left of *Heeresgruppe Mitte* was given to *Feldmarschall* Walther Model, known as Hitler's *fireman*. Model sent the *Totenkopf* division to the city of Grodno, and there it was ordered to hold the right flank of the *4.Armee* in the north, and the left wing of the *2.Armee* in the south. Here in the city of Grodno this crack *SS* division held onto its crumbling positions, fighting off continuous attacks amid bitter street fighting that was reminiscent of some of the close-quarter battles that had raged at Stalingrad. However, outnumbered seven to one in troop strength and ten to one in tanks, Totenkopf were gradually ground down in a battle of attrition, and by 18 July requested permission to abandon their receding lines. Model agreed at once and ordered the withdrawal of the division west in the retreat towards the Polish capital, Warsaw.

During the last week of July the Russians pushed forward and rolled across the ravaged countryside of Poland through the shattered German front. On 24 July in the southern sector of the front, the *1.Panzer-Armee* still held the town of Lwow and its front to the south. However, behind the Panzer army fifty miles west of Lwow massive Soviet forces were closing to the San River on the stretch between Jaroslaw and Przemysl. Further north in the centre Model had feverishly regrouped his forces in an attempt to defend Siedlce, Warsaw, and the Vistula south to Pulawy. The *Totenkopf* division was once again thrown into battle this time along with the elite armoured Paratroop Division, known as the *Herman Goring Fallschirmdivision.* Both divisions were ordered to hold the city of Siedlce fifty miles east of Warsaw. For four days in the face of strong Russian armoured strikes both divisions with great cost held their lines allowing the *2.Armee* to retreat to the Vistula River. On 28 July, they abandoned Siedlce and continued a fighting withdrawal towards Warsaw. Over the coming week fighting in the area was fierce, but both divisions fought to the bitter death, slowing the Russian onslaught and allowing Model to reorganise a defence along the river. As for the Soviet forces, having advanced another two hundred miles in two weeks, they had temporarily outstripped their supplies. The offensive ground to a halt on the Vistula in early August. The brief lull in fighting helped Model to gradually gain strength and reorganise defensive positions. The *Totenkopf* and the *Wiking* divisions formed the *IV.Panzer-Korps* commanded by *SS-Gruppenführer* Herbert Gille, and Model placed this *Korps* 30 miles northeast of Warsaw, where he expected the renewal of the Russian offensive.

Inside the capital, as news spread that the Russians were drawing closer, the Polish Home Army suddenly revolted and attempted to restore its Polish sovereignty against the German invaders. The Polish revolt surprised the German command and they quickly brought all available resources they could scrape together to combat the Polish attack. The notorious *Dirlewanger* and *Kaminski* brigades of *SS* irregulars were used against the Warsaw uprising. It was here in the ravaged streets of Warsaw that these *SS* units earned their terrible reputation for a string of atrocities. Here the soldiers were encouraged exploit the situation to the full and turn the streets into a bloodbath. Women and children were evacuated from their homes and herded together like animals. In cemeteries, gardens, and squares, the civilians were indiscriminately machine gunned until the frightened mass showed no further sign of life. Within four days of the battle, some 10,000 men, women, and children had been slaughtered in the city, but still the fighting continued.

Whilst the Warsaw uprising was being suppressed the Russians attacked on 14 August northwest of the city and, for several bloody days, the well dug-in *Waffen-SS* divisions of *Totenkopf* and *Wiking* grimly held out repulsing a number of viscous attacks. The Red Army then regrouped and once again resumed their attack, which fell on *Totenkopf.* For four days *SS* troops endured a gauntlet of heavy fighting. Russian air support hammered the German frontlines day and night until the *Totenkopf* and the remainder of the *Panzer-Korps* withdrew from its battered and blasted positions west towards Warsaw. By 10 September heavy fighting engulfed the suburbs of the city with *Totenkopf* successfully defending its positions. For ten days, until the Red Army offensive petered out, the *SS* managed to hold their lines, in spite of the high losses. During the next few weeks until 10 October there followed a lull in the fighting until the Russians launched yet another offensive, which forced the *IV.Panzer-Korps* to retreat 20 miles westwards. By 27 October the front had once more been stabilised and the Red Army abandoned further assaults against the *IV.Panzer-Korps.* Calm returned to the front around Warsaw and both *Wehrmacht* and *Waffen-SS* divisions tended to their wounded, reequipped the best they could and dug another defensive line. *Totenkopf's* performance in these defensive battles had demonstrated the effectiveness of using the *Waffen-SS* as a special 'fire brigade' force. They had not only fought off many attacks against an enemy sometime ten-times their strength, but had provided Model's soldiers with a band of men that were able to be rushed from one danger zone to another, plugging gaps in the front wherever they appeared. But the German military situation during the summer of 1944 had been a complete disaster in Poland. Although the Soviet advance had been relatively slow, continuously fighting against bitter opposition, the Germans were unquestionably stalling the inevitable defeat in a country that they had conquered and ravaged for almost five years.

Elsewhere on the Eastern Front the situation was equally dire. In the south Malinovsky's 2nd Ukrainian Front had broken through powerful German defences, and the Red Army reached the Bulgarian border in early September. Within a week, Russian troops reached the Yugoslav frontier, and on 8 September, Bulgaria and Romania declared war on Germany. By 23 September, Soviet forces arrived on the Hungarian border and immediately raced through the country for the Danube, finally reaching the river to the south of Budapest.

It was here in Hungary that Hitler placed the utmost importance of defending what he called the last bastion of defence in the East. Against all military logic, he felt that it was Hungary and not the Vistula River in Poland, which presented a natural barrier against an advance on Germany. For the defence of Hungary he was determined to use his premier *Waffen-SS* divisions, including *Totenkopf* and *Wiking* that were positioned along the Vistula River.

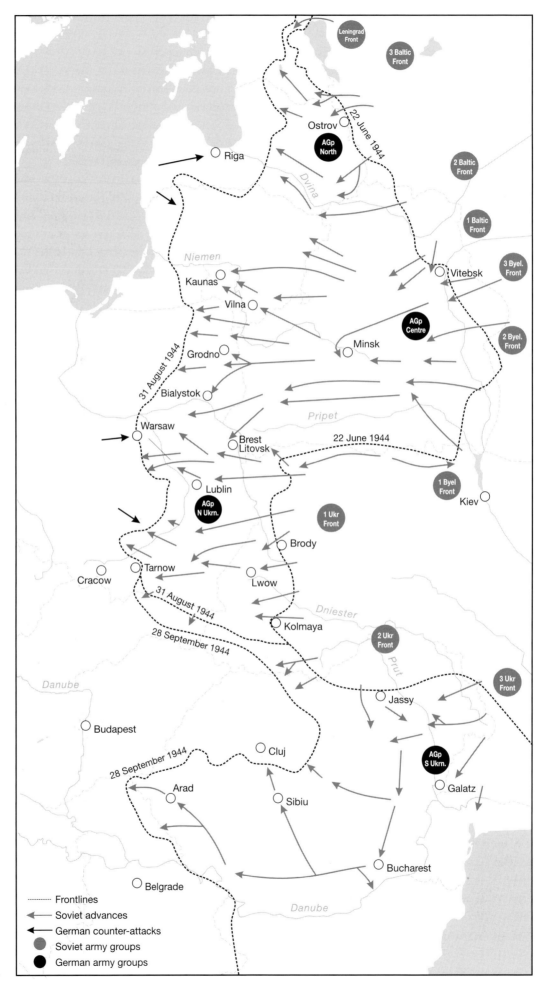

Map 5: Eastern Front, the Soviet Summer Offensives 1944

A group of *Totenkopf* soldiers pose for the camera in mid-June 1944 prior to the great Russia offensive codenamed Operation `Bagration`. During the spring and early summer of 1944 *Totenkopf* had been acting along with the 47.*Panzer-Korps* as an armoured rearguard, protecting the withdrawal of the 6.*Armee* through Romania, which took them to the foothills of the Carpathian Mountains.

Troops of the *Wiking* division in a crop field in Poland in the summer of 1944. The division had suffered heavy losses in the East and as result had withdrawn into Poland to take part in the defensive battles around Warsaw.

Well-camouflaged soldiers of the *Wiking* division east of Warsaw in July 1944. By this stage of the war the *Wikingers* had attained an elite status equal to the best of the original *Waffen-SS* divisions.

Troops of the *Wiking* division in a field east of Warsaw. By 1944 the qualities of the *Wiking* division as a combat unit were already testified by the number of Knight's Crosses of the Iron Cross awarded to its soldiers. A total of 54 such gallantry awards were made, a figure surpassed only by 73 for the *Das Reich* division.

Two *Wiking* soldiers casually chat during operations east of Warsaw in July 1944. Throughout the defensive fighting on the Eastern Front the men of the *Wiking* division fought like tigers and battled from one receding front to another.

A *Wiking* MG34 machine gun crew during a lull in defensive operations in Poland in the summer of 1944.

A rare photograph showing soldiers of the regimental battle group designated *Kampfgruppe SS-Polizei-Division*. This force fought in Russia on the Northern Front until it was disbanded in the summer of 1944.

Soldiers of the *Kampfgruppe SS-Polizei-Division* in the summer of 1944. The commanding officer is about to inspect his troops.

At a field depot in Poland the commander of a StuG.III can be seen sitting on the rim of the vehicle's cupola. Assault guns and self-propelled guns proved indispensable to the *Waffen-SS*, especially during the last months of the war.

Here *SS* troops are making full use of the extensive narrow gauge-railroads in the East. These specially adapted flatcars were much wider in proportion to the track than wider gauge rolling stock, and could carry surprisingly heavy loads.

A Sd.Kfz.7 halftrack towing a Pak 40 anti-tank gun attached to the *Totenkopf* division in eastern Poland in July 1944. By this period of the war the Red Army had already crossed the Polish frontier and was making an advance west towards Warsaw.

The *SS* commander of a well-concealed StuG.III Ausf.G peers through his binoculars whilst operating in Poland in the summer of 1944.

A 2cm quadruple-barrelled self-propelled anti-aircraft gun mounted on the back of a Sd.Kfz.7 halftrack advances along a road in the Balkans in October 1944. This flak unit belongs to the *Prinz Eugen* Division that was engaged during this time in anti-partisan duties.

A commanding officer of the *Prinz Eugen* Division discusses the location with two officers during anti-partisan operations in the Balkans. Note the officer on the left, who can be seen distinctively wearing the divisional insignia, the so-called *Odalrune* of the 7.*SS*, on his right collar.

A group of soldiers belonging to the *Prinz Eugen* Division march along a road during operations in the Balkans in October 1944. It was during this period that the division suffered heavy casualties around Belgrade.

Moving steadily westward back towards the borders of Poland is an Sd.Kfz.10 laden with *Waffen-SS* troops of the *Totenkopf* division. Due to the amount of heavy traffic in the area and the occasional downpour of rain, the road has been turned in a sea of mud.

Three StuG.III's in Poland in the summer of 1944 advance across a waterlogged field. These vehicles proved a valuable infantry support to both the *Wehrmacht* and *Waffen-SS*. However, by the late summer of 1944, a as the shortages of tanks grew, the StuGs were depended on more and more by the Panzer regiments.

Red Army soldiers have been captured by troops of the *Wiking* division east of Warsaw in July 1944.

A *Waffen-SS* Marder.III tank destroyer is stationary in a field in Poland in 1944. The tank commander sitting on the vehicle's left fender is reading a map.

Four Pz.Kpfw.IV tanks of the *Totenkopf* division are acting as a rearguard to the 6.Armee as it withdraws through Romania.

9. Hungary

In Hungary, the capital Budapest came under the direct command of General Otto Wöhler's *Heeresgruppe Süd*. Units committed to the defence of the Hungarian capital included the 22.*SS*.Freiwilligen-Kavallerie-Division *Maria Theresia* and 18.*SS*.Freiwilligen-Panzergrenadier-Division *Horst Wessel*. These *SS* forces were not only employed to protect Budapest, but were also there to retain law and order and suppress any local uprisings. However, in October 1944 as news reached the capital that the Red Army had crossed the Hungarian frontier and were advancing towards the Danube in the direction of Budapest, Hitler wasted no time and ordered his premier *SS* divisions to Hungary.

On 26 December, the *VI.Panzer-Korps*, comprising *Totenkopf* and *Wiking*, were transferred from the Warsaw area and given orders to relieve Budapest. The attack was scheduled to begin earnest on New Year's Day. Two attempts were made to relieve the city but the *VI.Panzer-Korps* was beaten back by strong Soviet forces. Consequently, for the next five weeks both *Totenkopf* and *Wiking* were forced onto the defensive and could only watch the beleaguered garrison struggled against large scale Red Army attacks. On 11 February the remaining *SS* troops trapped inside the city attempted to breakout to the west. In the terrible battles that ensued, the fleeing *SS* troops of *Florian Geyer* and *Maria Theresia* were virtually annihilated. Out of the 30,000 *SS* troops that tried to escape, only some 700 of them eventually reached the *VI.Panzer-Korps* lines. By 12 February Budapest was in Russian hands.

The remnants of both the two decimated *SS* foreign volunteer divisions were quickly absorbed to form the 37.*SS*.Freiwilligen-Kavallerie-Division *Lützow*. The *SS* division, which never even reached strength of a single regiment, was soon to be on the front lines fighting alongside the 6.*SS*.Panzer-Armee in a new plan aimed at retaking Budapest. The plan, code-named *Spring Awakening*, involved attacks by Wöhler's *Heeresgruppe Süd*, which would comprise of the 6.*SS*.Panzer-Armee, 8.Armee, 6.Armee and the Hungarian 3.Army. The German and Hungarian force would attack south from Margarethe defence lines, while *Heeresgruppe Süd-Ost 2.Armee* would attack from the west of the Russian lines. The planned pincer movement would crush the 3rd Ukrainian Front. As for the 6.*SS*.Panzer-Armee, they would remain the Margarethe positions around Lake Balaton. The *Panzer-Korps* was commanded by *SS-Oberstgruppenführer* Sepp Dietrich, and it consisted of the *Leibstandarte*, *Das Reich*, *Hohenstaufen* and *Hitlerjugend* divisions. These *SS* divisions were all newly arrived from the Ardennes offensive. However, they were not the same mighty *SS* combat formations that had fought previously in the East.

For the attack, the *Leibstandarte* and *Hitlerjugend* were grouped together to form the *I.SS.Panzer-Korps*, while *Das Reich* and *Hohenstaufen* formed the *II.SS.Panzer-Korps*. The operation was regarded so secret that even the *SS* commanders were not allowed to reconnoitre the areas in which their units would operate in case the enemy begun to suspect an operation was about to be mounted. All identifying *SS* insignia was also ordered to be removed and unit names were changed in a drastic effort to fool the Russians. However, when the *SS* undertook preliminary attacks, the Red Army finally detected a large body of elite *Waffen-SS* troops around the Lake Balaton area and quickly strengthened their defences by widening their mine belts and preparing antitank defences in depth. The Arctic conditions, too, in the area also helped the Russians, as they would make the *SS* advance more difficult to achieve.

During the early hours of the morning on 6 March 1945, *Operation Spring Awakening* was finally unleashed. Although total secrecy of the attack had been lost soldiers moving to the front were dropped off by their transport vehicles some twelve miles back from the launch point of their attack, and had to cover the remainder of the distance by foot. When they arrived at their launch point many of the *Waffen-SS* grenadiers were soaked, freezing and totally exhausted. In fact, in a number of areas many grenadiers had not even reached their assigned jump-off positions when the artillery barrage intended to soften up the Russian lines began at 0430 hours. Some commanders were so concerned about the state of their men arriving at the front that they requested for the attack to be postponed. However, these concerns were totally ignored. Instead, the grenadiers trudged out across the terrain through miserable conditions, reminiscent of fighting across the vast cold expanses of the Soviet Union. Because the area was marshy they were unable to be supported by armour and as a consequence were open to hostile fire. Although there were many losses in the *Panzer-Korps*, these were elite *SS* grenadiers and their élan soon brought them across a succession of enemy trench lines where they went onto capture a number of tactically important pieces of high ground. The *I.SS.Panzer-Korps* drove forward with great determination, driving the enemy back up to twenty-five miles in some places. The *II.SS.Panzer-Korps*, however, struggled against more bitter opposition and could only manage to penetrate the lines of some five miles.

Throughout the next few days of the operation the *Waffen-SS* battled its way slowly forward, in spite of the losses and damage to their precious remaining vehicles. By 13 March it was clear to *Heeresgruppe Süd* that the offensive was failing and that the Red Army were preparing to go over to the offensive.

The Russian offensive which *Heeresgruppe Süd* had forecast finally opened on 16 March. Along the whole front the initial blows of the Red Army were so severe that they were able to bring *Operation Spring Awakening* to an abrupt halt. Within hours of the artillery firestorm being unleashed onto the German positions, the *6.SS.Panzer-Armee* was in danger of being totally cut-off. The divisions of the *6.SS* tried desperately to fight on but were being slowly battered into the ground. *Das Reich* doggedly held open a corridor of escape for its comrades, but the defection of the Hungarian Army left the flanks wide open to the Russians. It did not take long before Operation Spring Awakening was routed, and its elite troops had to begin a full retreat, or face total annihilation. By 25 March, the Red Army had smashed its way through the German defences and wrenched open a gap more than sixty miles wide.

The shock waves of the *SS* failure in Hungary reverberated throughout Hitler's headquarters in Berlin. Joseph Goebbels' diary entry records:

> The *Führer* has decided to make an example of the *SS* formations. He has commissioned Himmler to fly to Hungary to remove their armbands.

Dietrich and his commanders were furious at this insult to the gallantry and self-sacrifice shown by his soldiers. He ordered that not one cuffband, which the soldiers of these elite units wore with such pride, was to be removed. The *Führer* headquarters had totally failed to recognise and understand the terrible conditions in Hungary and as a consequence the *SS* had lost the last vestiges of respect for their *Führer*. From now on they would be loyal to the *Waffen-SS* itself, to their own divisions and their commanders.

Within ten days of the Red Army opening its counter-offensive it had pushed its way through the Vertes mountains across three major rivers and had smashed to pieces the German formations opposing it. The speed of which the Russians conducted there operations in Hungary must have reminded the German commanders of the old days of *Blitzkrieg* – massed armour accompanied by masses of low-flying aircraft and dense waves of infantry that created and exploited the enemy lines.

By 2 April, the Russians had reached the Neusiedler Lake, on the border between Hungary and Austria, and two days later the last German defenders had been finally driven out of Hungary. Of the *Waffen-SS* divisions that had fought in Hungary, the bulk of them withdrew into Austria to defend Vienna. The *Leibstandarte*, now forming two *Kampfgruppen*, which held a line running from Vienna to Wiener Neustadt. *Das Reich* was also put into line to defend Vienna, before withdrawing into the city and becoming involved in bitter fighting. *Totenkopf*, too fought a defensive battle around the Austrian capital, while the *Hitlerjugend* withdrew into strong defensive positions around the Wienerwald, to the south west of the city. As for the *Hohenstaufen* division they were badly smashed to pieces during the battle around Vienna, and its pitiful remnants limped westwards to the Americans lines.

All the *SS* divisions put up largely symbolic resistance to the two huge Soviet fronts converging on the city. Although there were appeals that Vienna should be held at all costs Dietrich decided to withdraw his men to the west than face a massacre. On 13 April, the Red Army marched into the city.

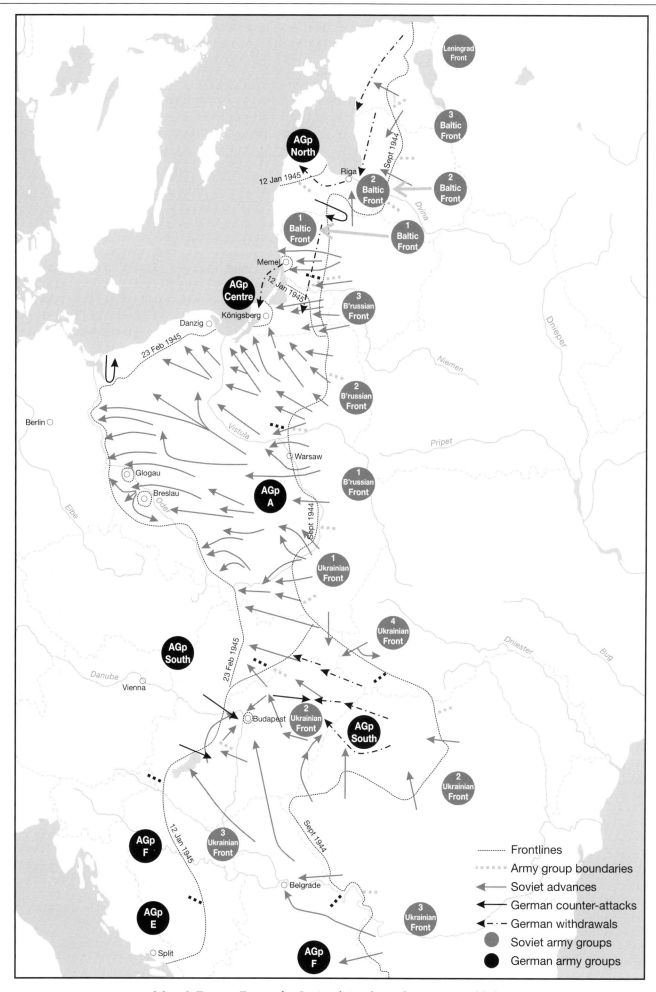

Map 6: Eastern Front, the Soviet drive through Europe 1944-45

A group of flak soldiers belonging to the *Leibstandarte*. This photograph was taken in Hungary in February 1945. The division formed part of the 6.*SS*.Panzer-Armee that consisted of the *Leibstandarte, Das Reich, Hohenstaufen,* and *Hitlerjugend*. All these troops had arrived from the abortive Ardennes offensive and no longer resembled the once mighty formations they had been.

Das Reich troops experience extreme difficulties in moving men and equipment through mud during operations in Hungary in early 1945.

A *Das Reich* artillery crew open fire on Red Army positions during Operation `Spring Awakening`. The main artillery barrage to soften up the Soviet positions began at 0430 hours on 6 March 1945.

StuG.III`s of the I.*SS*.Panzer-Korps move forward into action. Despite the losses in men and equipment the *Waffen-SS* threw themselves into the battle with all their customary élan and determination, driving the enemy back and advancing some 25 miles with their armour.

Waffen-SS grenadiers from the II.*SS*.Panzer-Korps prepare to advance alongside a Pz.Kpfw.IV during the initial phase of Operation `Spring Awakening`. Across the snow-covered terrain the II.*SS.Panzer-Korps* could only manage to penetrate around 5 miles into the enemy lines before coming to an abrupt stop.

Waffen-SS grenadiers from the I.*SS.Panzer-Korps* pass a burning Russian T-34 tank during the first morning of the attack against strong Soviet forces.

A *SS* MG34 machine gun crew utilise a captured motorboat to move rapidly across a small lake in order to set up a new defensive position.

Waffen-SS grenadiers from the *Das Reich* division receive two captured Russian prisoners during the first phase of the operation to relieve the Hungarian capital, Budapest.

A whitewashed StuG.III Ausf.G of the II.*SS*.Panzer-Korps prepares to move out and begin its advance with supporting grenadiers. The initial advance for the II.*SS*.Panzer-Korps did not go smoothly, and soon floundered in mud and ice. Almost immediately the *SS* attack suffered heavy losses.

Volunteer soldiers on the northern front. Most of the so called *Waffen-SS* crack divisions were still embroiled in heavy fighting in Hungary and were unable to be released in order to plug the massive gaps on the German front lines in the East. This left the northern and central sectors of the Eastern Front manned in many places by *SS* European volunteers.

10. Final Battles

In the last months of the war German forces continued receding across a scarred and devastated wasteland. On both the Western and Eastern Fronts, the last agonising moments of the war were played out. Whilst the British and American troops were poised to cross the River Rhine, in the East the terrifying advance of the Red Army was bearing down on the River Oder, pushing back the last remnants of Hitler's exhausted units. The resistance of her once mighty armies were now collapsing amid the ruins of the *Reich*. Most of the so called *Waffen-SS* crack divisions were still embroiled in heavy fighting in Hungary and were unable to be released in order to plug the massive gaps on the German front lines in the East. This left the northern and central sectors of the Eastern Front to eastern and western European *SS* volunteers. Many of the volunteers, spurred on by the worrying prospect of Russian occupation of Europe and certain death if captured, were determined to defend to the bitter end and try to hold back the Red Army advance.

The last great offensive that brought the Russians their final victory in the East began during the third week of January 1945. The principal objective was to crush the remaining German forces in Poland, East Prussia and the Baltic states. Along the Baltic an all-out Russian assault had begun in earnest with the sole intention to crush the remaining understrength German units that had once formed *Heeresgruppe Nord*. It was these heavy, sustained attacks that eventually restricted the German-held territory in the north-east to a few small pockets of land surrounding three ports: Libau in Kurland, Pillau in East Prussia and Danzig at the mouth of the River Vistula.

Here along the Baltic the German defenders attempted to stall the massive Russian push with the remaining weapons and men they had at their disposal. Every German soldier defending the area was aware of the significance if it was captured. Not only would the coastal garrisons be cut off and eventually destroyed, but also masses of civilian refugees would be prevented from escaping from those ports by sea. Hitler made it quite clear that all remaining *Wehrmacht, Waffen-SS* volunteer units, and *Luftwaffe* personnel were not to evacuate, but to stand and fight and wage an unprecedented battle of attrition. In fact, what Hitler had done by a single sentence was to condemn to death 8,000 officers and more than 181,000 soldiers and *Luftwaffe* personnel.

In southwest Poland, the strategic town of Breslau situated on the River Oder had been turned into a fortress and defended by various *Volkssturm, Hitlerjugend, Waffen-SS* and various formations from the 269.Infantry-Division. During mid-February 1945 the German units put up a staunch defence with every available weapon that they could muster. As the battle raged, both German soldiers and civilians were cut to pieces by Russian attacks. During these vicious battles, which endured until May 1945, there were many acts of courageous fighting. Cheering and yelling, old men and boys of the *Volkssturm* and *Hitlerjugend*, supported by *ad-hoc SS* units, advanced across open terrain, sacrificing themselves in front of well-positioned Russian machine gunners and snipers. By the first week of March, Russian infantry had driven back the defenders into the inner city and were pulverising it street by street. Lightly clad *SS, Volkssturm* and *Hitlerjugend* were still seen resisting, forced to fight in the sewers beneath the decimated city. When the defenders of Breslau finally capitulated almost 60,000 Russian soldiers had been killed or wounded trying to the capture the town, with some 29,000 German military and civilian casualties.

Elsewhere on the Eastern Front, fighting was merciless, with both sides imposing harsh measures on their men to stand where they were and fight to the death. In the *Wehrmacht* and *Waffen-SS* volunteer divisions, all malingerers were hanged by the roadside without even a summary court-martial. Those who deserted or caused self-inflicted wounds were executed on the spot. Soldiers would regularly pass groups of recently erected gallows, where the *SS* and *Feldgendarmerie* had hanged deserters. Signs were tied around their necks, some of them reading:

Here I hang because I did not believe in the *Führer*[1]

With every defeat and withdrawal came ever-increasing pressure on the commanders to exert harsher discipline on their weary men. The thought of fighting on German soil for the first time resulted in mixed feelings among the soldiers. Although the defence of the *Reich* automatically stirred emotional feelings to fight for their land, not all soldiers felt the same way. More and more young conscripts were showing signs that they did not want to die for a lost cause. Conditions on the Eastern Front were miserable not only for the newest recruits, but also for battle-hardened soldiers who had survived many months of bitter conflict against the Red Army. The cold harsh weather during February and March prevented the soldiers digging trenches more than a metre deep. But the main problems that confronted the German forces during this period were shortages of ammunition, fuel and vehicles. Some vehicles in a division could only be used in an emergency and battery fire was strictly prohibited without permission from the commanding officer. The daily ration on average per division was for two shells per gun.

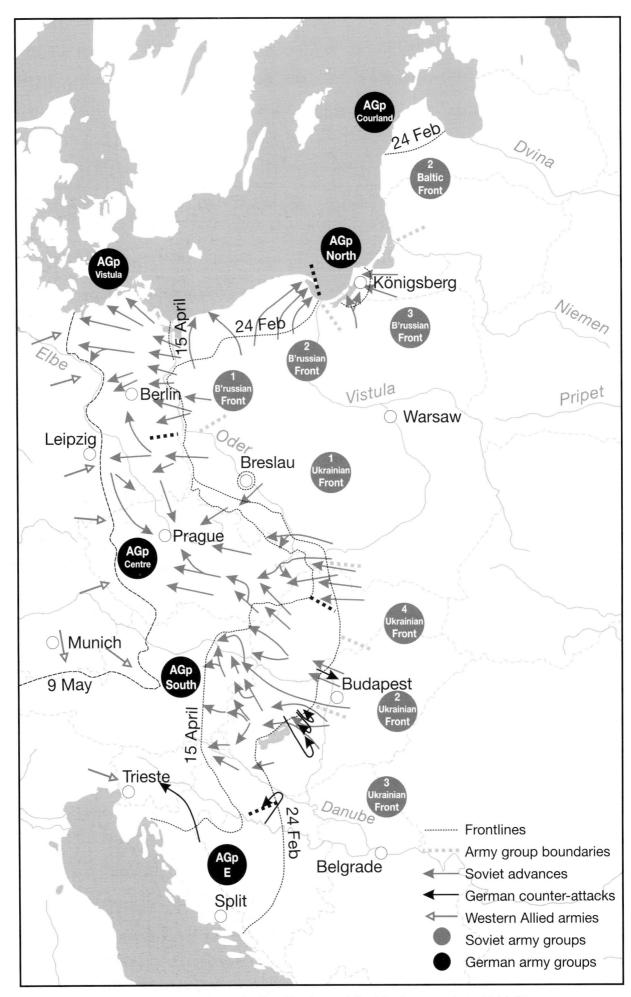

Map 7: Eastern Front, Berlin offensive and final Soviet operations 1944-45

With such drastic restrictions of every kind, tens of thousands of under-nourished civilians, mostly women, alongside remaining slave labourers, were marched out to expend all their available energy to dig lines of anti-tank ditches. Most of the ditches were dug between the Vistula and Oder Rivers, as a secondary line of defence. However, German forces were now barely holding the wavering Vistula positions that ran some 175 miles from the Baltic coast to the juncture of the Oder and Neisse in Silesia. Most of the front was now held on the western bank of the Oder. In the north, the ancient city of Stettin, capital of Pomerania, and in the south, the town of Küstrin, were both vital holding points against the main Russian objective of the war – Berlin.

As the great Red Army drive gathered momentum, more towns and villages fell to the onrushing forces. Suicidal opposition from a few *SS* and *Wehrmacht* strongpoints bypassed in earlier attacks reduced buildings to blasted rubble. Everywhere it seemed the Germans were being constantly forced to retreat. Many isolated units spent hours or even days fighting a bloody defence. Russian soldiers frequently requested them to surrender and assured them that no harm would come to them if they did so. But despite this reassuring tone, most German troops continued to fight to the bitter end. To the German soldier in 1945 they were fighting an enemy that they not only despised, but also were terrified of. Many soldiers, especially those fighting in the ranks of the *Waffen-SS* decided that their fate would be met out on the battlefield. To them they would rather bleed fighting on the grasslands of Eastern Europe than surrender and be at the mercy of a Russian soldier.

By the end of March, rations for the soldiers had become much worse. A Latvian *SS* volunteer belonging to the 15.*SS.Waffengrenadier*-Division der *SS* wrote:

> On most days we received an Army loaf and some stew or soup, which was often cold and not very appetising. The main problem was the lack of drinking water. As a result, many of us suffered from dysentery. Sitting in our stinking trenches, the faces of the men became gaunt from lack of sleep and their meagre diet. Most of the night they spent cowering under the constant Soviet shelling. Nobody dared move during daylight. Not only did we fear Russian aircraft attacks, but also snipers took a heavy toll.[2]

The bulk of the German forces that once consisted of *Heeresgruppe Mitte*, and was now know as *Heeresgruppe* Vistula were manned by many inexperienced training units. Some soldiers were so young that in their rations they had sweets instead of tobacco. All of them were ordered to stand and fight and not to abandon their positions. Terrified at the prospect of retreating, which would warrant almost certain execution if they did so, many reluctantly opted to bury themselves deep into a foxhole or bunker. Here they hoped the Soviet attackers would give them a chance to surrender, instead of burning them alive with flamethrowers or blowing them to pieces with hand grenades.

By early April the atmosphere among the troops of *Heeresgruppe* Vistula had become a mixture of terrible foreboding and despair as the Russians prepared to push forward on the River Oder. Here along the Oder and Neisse fronts the troops waited for the front to become engulfed by the greatest concentration of firepower ever amassed by the Russians. General Zhukov's 1st Belorussian Front and General Konev's 1st Ukrainian Front were preparing to attack German forces defending positions east of Berlin. For the attack the Red Army mustered some 2.5 million men, divided into four armies. They were supported by 41,600 guns and heavy mortars as well as 6,250 tanks and self-propelled guns.

The final battle before Berlin began at dawn on 16 April 1945. Just thirty-eight miles east of the German capital above the swollen River Oder, red flares burst into the night sky, triggering a massive artillery barrage. For nearly an hour, an eruption of flame and smoke burst along the German front. Then, in the mud, smoke, and darkness, the avalanche broke. In an instant, General Zhukov's soldiers were compelled to stumble forward into action. As they surged forward, the artillery barrage remained in front of them, covering the area ahead.

Under the cover of darkness on the night of 15th, most German forward units had been moved back to a second line just before the expected Russian artillery barrage. In this second line, as the first rays of light prevailed across the front, soldiers waited for the advancing Russians. Along the entire front, dispersed among the *3.* and *9.Armee's*, the Germans had fewer than 700 tanks and self-propelled guns. The strongest division, the 25.Panzer, had just 79 such vehicles: the weakest unit had just two. Artillery too was equally poor, with only 744 guns. Ammunition and fuel were in a critical state of supply and reserves in some units were almost non-existent. Opposing the main Russian assault stood the LVI.*Panzer-Korps*. It was under the command of General Karl Weidling, known to his friends as '*smasher Karl*'. Weidling had been given the awesome task of preventing the main Russian breakthrough in the area.

When the Soviet forces finally attacked during the early morning of 16 April, the Germans were ready to meet them on the Seelow Heights. From the top of the ridge, hundreds of German flak guns that had been hastily transferred from the Western Front poured a hurricane of fire into the enemy troops. All morning, shells and gunfire rained down on the Red Army, blunting their assault. By dusk the Russians, savagely mauled by the attack, fell back. It seemed the Red Army had under-estimated the strength and determination of their enemy.

By the next day, the Russians had still not breached the German defences. But General Zhukov, with total disregard of casualties, was determined to batter the enemy into submission and ruthlessly bulldoze his way through. Slowly and systematically the Red Army began smashing through their opponents. Within hours hard-pressed and exhausted German troops were feeling the full brunt of the assault. Confusion soon swept the decimated lines. Soldiers who had fought doggedly from one fixed position to another were now seized with panic.

In three days of constant fighting, thousands of German soldiers had perished. Despite their attempts to blunt the Red Army, the road to Berlin was finally wrenched wide open. At this crucial moment a number of top quality *SS* soldiers had been gathered in the recently established *11.Panzer-Armee* under the command of *SS-Obergruppenführer* Felix Steiner. The *11.Panzer-Armee* had been given the task of launching an offensive designed to dislocate the threatened enemy advance on Berlin, but had been halted against massive attacks. When the final push on Berlin began on 16 April, the *11.Panzer-Armee* retained only three reliable divisions. One of these, the 18.Panzergrenadier-Division, was transferred from east of Berlin. A few days later the 11.*SS.*Panzergrenadier-Division *Nordland* was rushed to Berlin and the *SS* Brigade *Nederland* was sent out of the capital to help stem the Russian advance. Inside the ruined city, part of the 15.*Waffengrenadier*-Division der *SS* from Latvia was ordered to take up defensive positions together with the Belgian *Langemarck* and *Wallonien* Divisions, and the remaining volunteers of the French *Charlemagne* Division. All of these *Waffen-SS* troops were to take part in the last, apocalyptic struggle to save the Reich capital from the clutches of the Red Army.

By 25 April Berlin was completely surrounded, and the next day some half a million Soviet troops bulldozed their way through the city. Beneath the *Reich* Chancellery building, which had now become Hitler's home and headquarters, the *Führer* was determined to save the crumbling capital and had already ordered remnants of *SS-Obergruppenführer* Felix Steiner's *11.Panzer-Armee* to attack immediately from their positions in the Eberswalde, then to drive south, cutting off the Russian assault on Berlin. On Hitler's map, the plan looked brilliant. But it was impossible to gather forces to make Steiner's *SS Kampfgruppe* even remotely operational. Steiner himself wrote that the forces at his disposal amounted to less than a weak *Korps*. He was well aware that his attack would receive little or no support as the *9.Armee* was completely surrounded and the *12.Armee* consisted only of a few battered divisions. As for Hitler's reinforcements they consisted of fewer than 5,000 *Luftwaffe* personnel and *Hitlerjugend,* all armed with hand-held weapons. The city was doomed.

For the next week the battle for Berlin raged. True to their motto, *My Honour is my Loyalty,* the *Waffen-SS* were seen fighting bitterly with members of the *Hitlerjugend, Volkssturm, Luftwaffe* and *Wehrmacht* troops. Here the soldiers were ordered to fight to the death and anyone found deserting or shirking from their duties were hunted down by *Reichsführer* Heinrich Himmler's personal Escort battalion and hanged from the nearest lamppost. But even in the last days of the war the *SS* proved to an efficient, formidable and ruthless fighting machine. Even as the last hours were fought out in the fiery cauldron of Berlin, *SS* units, lacking all provisions including many types of weapons, effectively halted and stemmed a number of Russian assaults.

Here *SS* volunteers are in action with a Pak 40 anti-tank gun during bitter fighting in the Baltic in early 1945. The principal objective of the Red Army was to crush the remaining German forces in Poland, East Prussia and the Baltic states. Along the Baltic an all-out Russian assault had begun in earnest with the sole intention to crush the remaining understrength German units that had once formed Heeresgruppe Nord.

Waffen-SS grenadiers huddle on the rear of a StuG.III. Ausf.G as German forces continue their slow withdrawal through East Prussia in early January 1945.

A *Waffen-SS* soldier stands along one of the ditches that were dug between the Vistula and Oder Rivers in March 1945. However, by this period of the war German forces were barely holding the meagre Vistula positions that ran some 175 miles from the Baltic coast to the juncture of the Oder and Neisse in Silesia. Most of the front was now held on the western bank of the Oder.

Exhausted *SS* volunteers withdraw through a deserted Baltic village in early 1945. Conditions on the Eastern Front were miserable not only for the newest recruits, but also for battle-hardened soldiers who had survived many months of bitter conflict against the Red Army.

SS troops inside a forest in late March 1945 west of the River Oder. By this period the atmosphere among the troops of Heeresgruppe Vistula became a mixture of terrible foreboding and despair as the mighty Red Army prepared to push forward on the River Oder.

A volunteer *SS* soldier with a camouflaged 8.8cm Flak gun near Kurland in January 1945. Here along the Baltic *Waffen-SS*, *Wehrmacht* and *Luftwaffe* personnel tried desperately to hold the last remaining small pockets of territory that were being slowly and inexorably engulfed by the Red Army.

Waffen-SS troops preparing defensive positions in February 1945. The cold harsh weather during February and March prevented the soldiers digging trenches more than a metre down. But the main problems that confronted the German forces during this period were shortages of ammunition, fuel and vehicles

SS troops in early April 1945. The men are armed with the MP38/40 sub-machine gun.

A Sd.Kfz.7 halftrack towing a Pak 40 anti-tank gun on the way to the receding front lines in early April 1945. By the last weeks of the war ammunition and fuel were in a critical state of supply and reserves in some units were almost non-existent.

A StuG assault gun, which still retains its coating of winter whitewash paint advances towards the Oder in March 1945. The River Oder was just thirty-eight miles east of the German capital, Berlin.

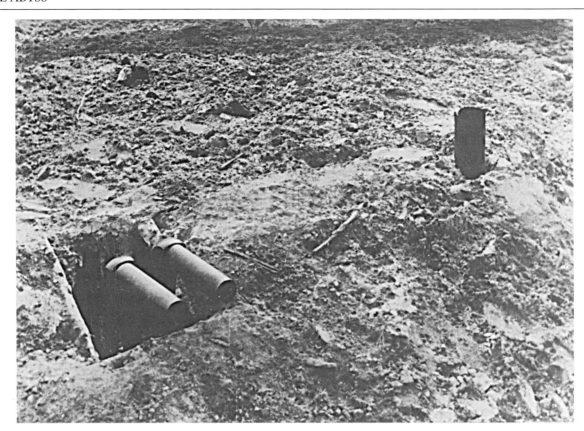

A pair of scissor binoculars has been well-camouflaged in position on the River Oder in March 1945. It was here along the Oder and Neisse fronts that *Waffen-SS, Wehrmacht, Luftwaffe* personnel, *Volkssturm* and *Hitlerjugend* troops waited for the front to become engulfed by the greatest concentration of firepower ever amassed by the Russians.

As the great Red Army drive gathered momentum, more towns and villages fell to the onrushing forces. Suicidal opposition from a few *SS* and *Wehrmacht* strongpoints bypassed in earlier attacks reduced buildings to blasted rubble. Everywhere it seemed the Germans were being constantly forced to retreat. Here in this photograph dejected *Waffen-SS* and *Wehrmacht* soldiers shuffle pass a stationary PzKpfw.IV during its withdrawal from the East in Germany in March 1945. Many isolated units spent hours or even days fighting a bloody defence and were slowly ground down by the sheer superiority of the Soviet colossus.

Epilogue

By the spring of 1945, the bulk of the premier *Waffen-SS* divisions were carrying out a fighting withdrawal through Hungary and Austria, while on the receding Eastern Front those *SS* units still in action were principally European volunteer units. Even by this late stage of the war the level of determination and courage shown by both first and second rate *SS* combat formations was quite exceptional, considering many soldiers were totally aware that there was no prospect of victory. However, in the closing days of the war most *Waffen-SS* soldiers were determined to withdraw west and surrender to the Anglo-American forces rather than the Red Army. Few of them harboured any illusions as to the kind of treatment that they would receive from the Russians. It was for this reason that the divisions of the once-vaunted *SS* decided to chance their luck in the west. The *Leibstandarte* surrendered to American forces at Seyr in Austria along with the remnants of *Hohenstaufen*. The *Totenkopf* capitulated to the Americans on 9 May, after withdrawing its forces northwest of Vienna. However, their relief of escaping the Red Army was short-lived as the Americans soon handed over the *Totenkopf* to the Soviets, who had a score to settle with this particular division. Very few of the soldiers survived Russian captivity.

Remnants of *Das Reich* were in the area of Dresden frantically trying to defend the region from Russian forces swarming into the *Reich*. Some elements of the division capitulated to Russian forces, whilst another major grouping finished the war fighting against the American Army in Austria, while a third group had been involved in a Prague rescue mission, until they too surrendered to other US units in the border region of western Czechoslovakia.

Whilst most of the remaining premier *Waffen-SS* divisions were captured, most of the foreign volunteers did not survive on the battlefields of Eastern Europe. The *Wiking* division, with its predominantly western European troops, were annihilated whilst fighting outside Vienna. *Nordland* was decimated during the battle of Berlin. The 14. *Waffengrenadier*-Division der *SS* surrendered in Czechoslovakia to Russian forces, and most of the surviving elements were summarily executed. Part of the 15. *Waffengrenadier*-Division der *SS* was slaughtered in Berlin. *Horst Wessel* with its Hungarian volunteers, surrendered to the Red Army near Prague. The 20. *Waffengrenadier*-Division der *SS* also capitulated near Prague, with many of the surviving soldiers being executed on the spot. The *Maria-Theresia* division was destroyed in its homeland fighting for Budapest. The 25. and 26. *Waffengrenadier*-Divisions also fell into Russian hands in Hungary. *Nederland* was smashed to pieces during the last stages of the battle of Berlin, and the remnants of the *Langemarck* and *Wallonien* divisions were also totally destroyed during the battle for *Reich* capital, as were the volunteers of the French *Charlemagne* division. The 30. *Waffengrenadier*-Division were also destroyed and its remnants were transferred to General Andrei Vlassov's Free Russian Army, but they were soon in embroiled in heavy fighting and fell into Red Army hands.

Although by early May 1945, the *Waffen-SS* was all but destroyed, in the eyes of the *SS* soldiers that marched into captivity, they had laid down their arms in the sound knowledge that no military formation in history had achieved more. They had battled across half Russia, they had shown their skill and endurance at Kursk and Kharkov, and gone on to protect the withdrawals of the rest of the German Army to the very gates of Berlin, and beyond.

Nobody could deny that these men, in their brief and extraordinary existence, had won a reputation for their skill and gallantry in combat. Throughout the war each *SS* soldier had looked upon himself as part of an elite fighting machine that was superior to that of his *Wehrmacht* counterpart. Even in defeat, as many frightened and dispirited Army troops shuffled off to the prisoner-of-war camps, the *SS* soldiers retained a measure of their arrogance and defiance, despite their beloved *Führer* sending them and their country into an abyss.

APPENDIX I

Waffen-SS Divisions Order of Battle 1943–1945

Publisher's note: divisional components have only been provided for some of the more major SS divisions, who feature heavily in the narrative of this book. The best single volume treatment of the organisation of the Waffen SS remains Dr K.-G. Klietmann, *Die Waffen-SS, eine Dokumentation,* published by Verlag Der Freiwillige, Osnabrück, 1965.

1.SS-Panzer-Division Leibstandarte Adolf Hitler

General Composition:

1943

SS-Grenadier-Regiment 1
SS-Grenadier-Regiment 2
Panzer-Regiment 1
Sturmgeschütz-Abteilung
Aufklärürungs-Abteilung
Artillerie-Regiment
Panzerjäger-Abteilung
Flak-Abteilung
Pionier-Bataillon
Nachrichten-Abteilung
Wirtschafts-Bataillon
Sanitäts-Abteilung
Nachschub-Deinst
Instandsetzungs-Abteilung
VII.LSSAH

1944

Stab der Division
SS-Panzer-Grenadier-Regiment 1
SS-Panzer-Grenadier-Regiment 2
SS-Panzer-Aufklärungs-Abteilung 1
SS-Panzerjäger-Abteilung
SS-Panzer-Artillerie-Regiment
SS-Flak-Abteilung 1
SS-Panzer-Pionier-Bataillon
SS-Panzer-Nachrichten-Abteilung

Area of Operations:

Early 1943 – France (Refit)
Late 1943 – France (Refit)
June 1944 – Normandy
December 1944 – Ardennes
February 1945 – Hungary

Commanders:

Oberstgruppenfüuhrer Joseph (Sepp) Dietrich, 1933 – 4.7.43
Brigadeführer Theodor Wisch, 4.7.43 – 20.8.44
Brigadeführer Wilhelm Mohnke, 20.8.44 – 6.2.45
Brigadeführer Otto Kumm, 6.2.45 – 8.5.45

2.SS-Panzer-Division Das Reich

General Composition:

SS-Standarte Germania (Removed from Division November, 1940)
3.SS-Panzergrenadier-Regiment Deutschland
4.SS-Panzergrenadier-Regiment Der Fuhrer
SS-Infanterie-Regiment Langemarck (Removed Summer, 1943)
SS-Infanterie-Regiment 11 (Disbanded November, 1940)
2.SS-Panzer-Regiment
2.SS-Panzerjäger-Abteilung
2.SS-Sturmgeschutz-Abteilung
2.SS-Panzer-Artillerie-Regiment
2.SS-Flak-Abteilung
2.SS-Werfer-Abteilung
2.SS-Panzer-Nachrichten-Abteilung
2.SS-Panzer-Aufklarungs-Abteilung
2.SS-Panzer-Pionier-Batallion
2.SS-Kradschutzen-Batallion
2.SS-Dina
2.SS-Feldlazarett
2.SS-Kriegsberichter-Zug
2.SS-Feldgendarmerie-Trupp
2.SS-Feldersatz-Battilon

Area of Operations:

Early 1943 – France
February 1943 – Southern Russia
Early 1944 – France
July 1944 – Normandy
December 1944 – Ardennes
February 1945 – Hungary
May 1945 – Bohemia

Commanders:

Obergruppenführer George Keppler, 19.4.42 – 10.2.43
Brigadeführer Hebert-Ernst Vahl, 10.2.43 – 18.3.43
Oberführer Kurt Brasack, 18.3.43 – 29.3.43
Obergruppenführer Walter Krüger, 29.3.43 – 23.10.43
Gruppenführer Heinz Lammerding, 23.10.43 – 24.7.44
Standartenführer Christian Tychsen, 24.7.44 – 28.7.44
Brigadeführer Otto Baum, 28.7.44 – 23.10.44
Gruppenführer Heinz Lammerding, 23.10.44 – 20.1.45
Standartenführer Karl Kreutz, 20.1.45 – 29.1.45
Gruppenführer Werner Ostnedorff, 20.1.45 – 9.3.45
Standartenführer Rudolf Lehmann, 9.3.45 – 13.4.45
Standartenführer Karl Kreutz, 13.4.45 – 8.5.45

3.SS-Panzer-Division Totenkopf

General Composition:

5.SS-Panzergrenadier-Regiment Thule
6.SS-Panzergrenadier-Regiment Theodor Eicke
2 SS-Totenkopf-Infanterie-Regiment 4 (Disbanded in Autumn, 1942)
3.SS-Panzer-Regiment
3.SS-Panzer-jager-Abteilung
3.SS-Sturmgeschutz-Abteilung
3.SS- (Panzer-) Artillerie-Regiment
3.SS-Flak-Abteilung
3.SS-Werfer-Abteilung
3.SS- (Panzer-) Nachrichten-Abteilung
3.SS-Panzer-Aufklarungs-Abteilung
3.SS-Panzer-Pionier-Batallion
3.SS-Dina
3.SS-Feldlazarett, etc
3.SS-Kriegsberichter-Zug
3.SS-Feldgendarmerie-Trupp
3.SS-Feldersatz-Battillon
SS-Heimwehr-Danzig
Freikorps Danmark

Area of Operations:

January 1943 – France
March 1943 – Eastern Front
April 1944 – Ukraine
July 1944 – Poland
February 1945 – Hungary
April/May 1945 – Austria

Commanders 1943 – 1945

Obergruppenführer Theodor Eicke, 19.9.41 – 26.2.43
Obergruppenführer Herman Priess, 26.2.43 – 27.4.43
Gruppenführer Heinz Lammerding, 27.4.43 – 15.5.43
Gruppenführer Max Simon, 15.5.43 – 22.10.43
Obergruppenführer Herman Priess, 22.10.43 – 21.6.44
Brigadeführer Helmut Becker, 21.6.44 – 8.5.45

4.SS-Polizei-Panzergrenadier-Division

General Composition:

SS-Panzer-Grenadier-Regiment 7
SS-Panzer-Grenadier-Regiment 8
SS-Panzer-Abteilung 4
SS-Panzerjäger-Abteilung 4
SS-Sturmgeschütz-Abteilung 4
SS-Artillerie-Regiment 4
SS-Flak-Abteilung 4
SS-Nachrichten-Abteilung 4
SS-Panzer-Aufklärungs-Abteilung 4
SS-Pionier-Bataillon 4
SS-Dina 4
SS-Panzer-Instandsetzungs-Abteilung 4
SS-Wirtschafts-Bataillon 4
SS-Sanitäts-Abteilung 4
SS-Polizei-Veterinar-Kompanie 4
SS-Kriegsberichter-Zug 4
SS-Feldgendarmerie-Trupp 4
SS-Feldersatz-Battillon 4

Area of Operations:

February 1943 – Leningrad
August 1944 – Yugoslavia
September 1944 – Ukraine
October 1944 – Hungary
March/April 1945 – West Prussia

Commanders:

Generaloberst der Polizei Alfred Wünnenberg, 15.12.41 – 17.4.43
Brigadeführer Fritz Freitag, 17.4.43 – 1.6.43
Brigadeführer Fritz Schmedes, 1.6.43 – 18.8.43
Brigadeführer Fritz Freitag, 18.8.43 – 20.10.43
Oberführer Friedrich-Wilhelm Bock, 20.10.43 – 19.4.44
Brigadeführer Jürgen Wagner, 19.4.44 – ??.5.44
Oberführer Friedrich-Wilhelm Bock, ??.5.44 – 5.7.44
Brigadeführer Hebert-Ernst Vahl, 5.7.44 – 22.7.44
Standartenführer Karl Schümers, 22.7.44 – 16.8.44
Oberführer Helmuth Dörnder, 16.8.44 – 22.8.44
Brigadeführer Fritz Schmedes, 22.8.44 – 27.11.44
Standartenführer Walter Harzer, 27.11.44 – 1.3.45
Standartenführer Fritz Göhler, 1.3.45 – ??.3.45
Standartenführer Walter Harzer, ??.3.45 – 8.5.45

5.SS-Panzer-Division Wiking

General Composition:

SS-Panzer-Grenadier-Regiment 9 Germania
SS-Panzer-Grenadier-Regiment 10 Westland
SS-Panzer-Grenadier-Regiment Nordland (Withdrawn from division in 1943)
Estnische SS-Freiwilligen-Panzer-Grenadier-Batallion 'Narwa' (Withdrawn in 1944)

Finnisches Freiwilligen-Batallion der Waffen-SS
SS-Sturmbrigade Wallonien
SS-Panzer-Regiment 5
SS-Panzerjäger-Abteilung 5
SS-Sturmgeschütz-Abteilung 5
SS-Sturmgeschütz-Batterie 5
SS-Panzer-Artillerie-Regiment 5
SS-Flak-Abteilung 5
SS-Werfer-Abteilung 5
SS-Panzer-Nachrichten-Abteilung 5
SS-Panzer-Aufklärungs-Abteilung 5
SS-Panzer-Pionier-Batallion 5
SS-Dina 5
SS-Instandsetzungs-Abteilung 5
SS-Wirtschafts-Batallion 5
SS-Sanitäts-Abteilung 5
SS-Feldlazarett 5
SS-Kriegsberichter-Zug 5
SS-Feldgendarmerie-Trupp 5
SS-Feldersatz-Batillon 5
I./SS-Panzer-Grenadier-Regiment 23 Norge
I./SS-Panzer-Grenadier-Regiment 24 Danmark

Area of Operations:

January 1943 – Eastern Front Don River
March 1943 – Southern Russia
April 1944 – Central Russia
August 1944 – Poland
January 1945 – Hungary
May 1945 – Austria

Commanders:

Obergruppenführer Felix Steiner, 1.12.40 – 1.5.43
Obergruppenführer Herbert Gille, 1.5.43 – 6.8.44
Oberführer Edmund Deisenhofer, 6.8.44 – ??.8.44
Standartenführer Rudolf Mühlenkamp, ??.8.44 – 9.10.44
Oberführer Karl Ulrich, 9.10.44 – 5.5.45

6.SS-Gebirgs-Division Nord

General Composition:

Stab der Division
SS-Gebirgs-Jäger-Regiment 11 Reinhardt Heydrich
SS-Gebirgs-Jäger-Regiment 12 Michael Gaissmair
SS-Panzer-Grenadier-Abteilung 506
SS-Infanterie-Regiment (mot) 5
SS-Infanterie-Regiment 9 (Removed from Division in 1943)
SS-Schützen-Abteilung (mot) 6
SS-(Gebirgs-) Panzerjäger-Abteilung 6
SS-Sturmgeschütz-Batterie 6
SS-Gebirgs-Artillerie-Regiment 6
SS-Flak-Abteilung 6
SS-(Gebirgs-) Nachrichten-Abteilung (mot?) 6
SS-Gebirgs-Aufklärungs-Abteilung (mot) 6
SS-(Gebirgs-) Pionier-Abteilung 6
SS-Ski-Jäger-Abteilung Norwegen or Norge

SS-Dina 6
SS-Bekleidungs-Instandsetzungs-Kompanie 6
SS-Sanitäts-Kompanie 6
SS-Veterinar-Kompanie 6
SS-Kriegsberichter-Zug 6
SS-Feldgendarmerie-Trupp 6
SS- Og Politikompani

Area of Operations:

January 1943-November 1944 – Finland/Norway
March/April 1945 – Germany

Commanders:

Obergruppenführer Matthias Kleinheisterkamp, 14.6.42 – 15.10.43
Gruppenführer Luther Debes, 15.10.43 – 14.6.43
Obergruppenführer Friedrich-Wilhelm Krüger, 14.6.43 – 23.8.44
Brigadeführer Gustav Lombard, 23.8.44 – 1.9.44
Gruppenführer Karl Brenner, 1.9.44 – 3.4.45
Standartenführer Franz Schreiber, 3.4.45 – 8.5.45

7.SS-Freiwilligen-Gebirgs-Division Prinz Eugen

General Composition:

SS Mountain Infantry Regiment 1
SS Mountain Infantry Regiment 2
SS Motorcycle Battalion
SS Cavalry Battalion
SS Panzer Battalion
SS Mountain Artillery Regiment
SS Engineer Battalion
SS Intelligence Battalion
SS Mountain Jäger Replacement Battalion
Supply troops

Later, the following were added:
SS Reconnaissance Battalion
SS Panzerjager Battalion
SS Motorcycle Rifle Battalion
SS Flak Unit

Its final composition was as follows:
SS Volunteer Mountain Jäger Regiment 13 Arthur Phelps
SS Volunteer Mountain Jäger Regiment 14 Skanderbeg
SS Volunteer Mountain Artillery Regiment 7
SS Panzer Unit 7
SS Panzer Company
SS Mountain Panzerjager Unit 7
SS Cavalry Unit 7
SS Assault Gun Battery 7
SS Flak Unit 7
SS Flak Company
SS Mountain Intelligence Unit 7
SS Volunteer Mountain Reconnaissance Unit 7 (mot)
SS Panzer Reconnaissance Platoon
SS Cycle Battalion

SS Cycle Reconnaissance Unit 7
SS Mountain Engineer Battalion
SS Mountain Rifle Battalion
SS Supply Company 7
SS Repair Shop Company/Platoon
SS Storekeeping Battalion 7
SS Medical Unit 7
SS Volunteer Mountain Veterinary Company 7
SS Volunteer Mountain Intelligence Platoon 7
SS Propaganda Platoon
SS Field Police Platoon 7
SS Field Replacement Battalion 7
SS Repair Unit 7
SS Geological Battalion

Area of Operations:

January 1943 until 1945 – Yugoslavia

Commanders:

Obergruppenführer Arthur Phelps, 30.1.42 – 15.5.43
Brigadeführer Karl Reichsritter von Oberkamp, 15.5.43 – 30.1.44
Brigadeführer Otto Kumm, 30.1.44 – 20.1.45
Brigadeführer August Schmidt Huber, 20.1.45 – 8.5.45

8.SS-Kavallerie-Division Florian Geyer

Formation name changes:

SS-Kavallerie-Brigade
SS-Kavallerie-Division
8.SS-Kavallerie-Division
8.SS-Kavallerie-Division Florian Geyer

Area of Operations:

January 1943 – Russian Central Front
September 1943 – Russian Southern Front
October 1943 – Hungary (Occupation Duties)
April 1944 – Yugoslavia
September 1944 – Ukraine
October 1944 – February 1945 – Hungary

Commanders:

Obergruppenführer Willi Bittrich, ??.8.42 – 15.2.43
Brigadeführer Fritz Freitag, 15.2.43 – 20.4.43
Brigadeführer Gustav Lombard, 20.4.43 – 14.5.43
Gruppenführer Hermann Fegelein, 14.5.43 – 13.9.43
Gruppenführer Bruno Streckenbach, 13.9.43 – 22.10.43
Gruppenführer Herman Fegelein, 22.10.43 – 1.1.44
Gruppenführer Bruno Streckenbach, 1.1.44 – 14.4.44
Brigadeführer Gustav Lombard, 14.4.44 – 1.7.44
Brigadeführer Joachim Rumohr, 1.7.44 – 11.2.45

9.SS-Panzer-Division Hohenstaufen

General Composition:

19.SS-Panzergrenadier-Regiment
20.SS-Panzergrenadier-Regiment

9.SS-Panzer-Regiment
9.SS-Artillerie-Regiment
9.SS-Aufklarung-Abteilung
9.SS-Panzerjäger-Abteilung
9.SS-Flak-Abteilung
9.SS-Pioneer-Abteilung
9.SS-Panzer-Nachrichten-Abteilung
9th SS Divisional Support Units

(The division's original 1.SS and 2.SS Panzergrenadier-Regiments were renamed as the 19.SS and 20.SS Panzergrenadier-Regiments on 10.23.43)

Area of Operations:

January 1943 – France
April 1944 – Ukraine
July 1944 – Normandy
September 1944 – Holland
December 1944 – Ardennes
February/April 1945 – Hungary

Commanders:

Obergruppenführer Willi Bittrich, 15.2.43 – 29.6.44
Oberführer Thomas Müller, 29.6.44 – 10.7.44
Brigadeführer Sylvester Stadler, 10.7.44 – 31.7.44
Oberführer Friedrich-Wilhelm Bock, 31.7.44 –29.8.44
Standartenführer Walter Harzer, 29.8.44 – 10.10.44
Brigadeführer Sylverster Stadler, 10.10.44 – 8.5.45

10.SS-Panzer-Division Frundsberg

General Composition:

June 1943

1.SS-Panzergrenadier-Regiment Frundsberg
2.SS-Panzergrenaider-Regiment Frundsberg
10.SS-Panzer-Regiment
10.SS-Kradschutzen-Regiment
SS Sturmgeschütz-Abteilung
SS Panzerjäger-Abteilung
SS Flak-Abteilung
SS Pioneer-Abteilung
SS Panzer-Nachrichten-Abteilung
10th SS Divisional Support Units

October 1943

21.SS-Panzergrenadier-Regiment
22.SS-Panzergrenadier-Regiment
10.SS-Panzer-Regiment
10.SS-Aufklarung-Abteilung
10.SS-Panzerjäger-Abteilung
10.SS-Flak-Abteilung
10.SS-Pioneer-Abteilung
10.SS-Panzer-Nachrichten-Abteilung
10th SS Divisional Support Units

(In October, 1943, this division was given the number 10 and was given official title of Frundsberg, while the 1st and 2nd SS-Panzergrenadier-Regiments were renumbered as the 21st and 22nd Panzergrenadier-Regiments)

Area of Operations:

January 1943 – Southern France
November 1943 – Northern France
April 1944 – Ukraine
July 1944 – Normandy
September 1944 – Holland
December 1944 – Belgium
February/April 1945 – Germany

Commanders:

Standartenführer Michael Lippert, ??.3.43 – 15.2.43
Gruppenführer Luther Debes, 15.2.43 – 15.11.43
Gruppenführer Karl Fischer von Treuenfeld, 15.11.43 – 27.4.44
Gruppenführer Heinz Harmel, 27.4.44 – ??.4.45
Obersturmbannführer Franz Roestel, ??.4.45 – 8.5.45

11.SS-Panzergrenadier-Freiwilligen-Division Nordland

Area of Operations:

September 1943 – Yugoslavia
December 1943 – Leningrad
March 1944 – Narva
November 1944 – Pomerania
April/May 1945 – Germany

Commanders:

Brigadeführer Franz Augsberger, 22.3.43 – 1.5.43
Gruppenführer Fritz Scholz, Elder von Rarancze, 1.5.43 – 27.7.44
Brigadeführer Joachim Ziegler, 27.7.44 – 25.4.45
Brigadeführer Dr. Gustav Krukenberg, 25.4.45 – 8.5.45

12.SS-Panzer-Division Hitlerjugend

General Composition:

July 1943

1.SS-Panzergrenadier-Regiment Hitlerjugend
2.SS-Panzergrenadier-Regiment Hitlerjugend
12.SS-Panzer-Regiment
12.SS-Artillerie-Regiment
12.SS-Kradschutzen-Regiment
12.SS-Aufklarung-Abteilung
12.SS-Kradschutzen-Regiment
12.SS-Panzerjäger-Abteilung
12.SS-Werfer-Abteilung
12.SS-Flak-Abteilung
12.SS-Pioneer-Abteilung
12.SS-Panzer-Nachrichten-Abteilung
12th SS Divisional Support Units

October 1943

25.SS-Panzergrenadier-Regiment Hitlerjugend
26.SS-Panzergrenadier-Regiment Hitlerjugend
12.SS-Panzer-Regiment
12.SS-Artillerie-Regiment
12.SS-Kradschutzen-Regiment
12.SS-Aufklarung-Abteilung
12.SS-Kradschutzen-Regiment
12.SS-Panzerjäger-Abteilung
12.SS-Werfer-Abteilung
12.SS-Flak-Abteilung
12.SS-Pioneer-Abteilung
12.SS-Panzer-Nachrichten-Abteilung
12th SS Divisional Support Units

Area of Operations:

July 1944 – Normandy
September 1944 – Belgium
January 1945 – Ardennes
February 1945 – Hungary
May 1945 – Austria

Commanders:

Brigadeführer Fritz de Witt, 24.6.43 – 14.6.44
Brigadeführer Kurt Meyer, 14.14.44 – 06.9.44
Obersturmbannführer Hubert Meyer, 06.9.44 – 24.10.44
Brigadeführer Fritz Kraemer, 24.10.44 – 13.11.44
Brigadeführer Hugo Kraas, 13.11.44 – 08.5.45

13.Waffen-Gebirgs-Division der SS Handschar (kroat.Nr.1)

Formation name changes:

Kroatische-SS-Freiwilligen-Division
Kroatische SS-Freiwilligen-Gebirgs-Division
13.SS-Freiwilligen-bosn.herzogow.Gebrigs-Division (Kroatien)
13.Waffen-Gebrigs-Division der SS Handschar (Kroatische Nr.1)

Area of Operations:

January 1944 – Yugoslavia
December 1944 – April 1945 – Hungary

Commanders:

Oberführer Herbert von Obwurzer, 1.4.43 – 9.8.43
Gruppenführer Karl-Gustav Sauberzweig, 9.8.43 – ??.6.44
Brigadeführer Desiderius Hampel, ??.6.44 – ??.9.44
??, ??.9.44 – ??.1.45
Brigadeführer Desiderius Hampel, ??.1.45 – 8.5.45

14.Waffen-Grenadier-Division der SS (Ukrainische Nr.1)

Formation name changes:

SS-Freiwilligen-Division Galizien
14.Galizische SS-Freiwilligen-Division
14.Galizische SS-Freiwilligen-Infanterie-Division

14.Waffen-Grenadier-Division der SS (Galizische Nr.1)
14.Waffen-Grenadier-Division der SS (Ukrainische Nr.1)

Area of operations:

July 1944 – Ukraine
April 1945 – Austria

Commanders:

Gruppenführer Walther Schimana, 30.6.43 – 20.11.43
Brigadeführer Fritz Freitag, 20.11.43 – 22.4.44
Brigadeführer Sylvester Stadler, 22.4.44 – ??.7.44
Brigadeführer Nikolaus Heilmann, ??.7.44 – 5.9.44
Brigadeführer Fritz Freitag, 5.9.44 – 24.4.45
Brigadeführer Pavlo Schandruk, 24.4.45 – 8.5.45

15. Waffen-Grenadier-Division der SS (lett.Nr.1)

Formation name changes:

Lettische SS-Freiwilligen Legion
Lettische SS-Freiwilligen-Division
15.Lettische SS-Freiwilligen-Division
15.Waffen-Grenadier-Division der SS (Lettische Nr.1)

Area of Operations:

December 1943 – Russian Northern Front
February 1945 – West Prussia
March 1945 – Kurland

Commanders:

Brigadeführer Peter Hansen, 25.2.43 – ??.5.43
Gruppenführer Carl Graf von Pückler-Burghauss, ??.5.43 – 17.2.44
Brigadeführer Nikolas Heilmann, 17.2.44 – 21.7.44
Brigadeführer Herbert von Obwurzer, 21.7.44 – 26.1.44
Oberführer Dr. Eduard Deisenhoffer, 26.1.45
Oberführer Arthur Ax, 26.1.45 – 15.2.45
Oberführer Karl Burk, 15.2.45-??.??.45

16.SS-Panzergrenadier-Division Reichsführer SS

Formation name changes:

Begleit-Bataillone Reichsführer SS
Sturmbrigade 'Reichsführer SS'
16.SS-Panzergrenadier-Division Reichsführer SS

Area of Operations:

June 1944 – Italy
February 1945 – Hungary
April/May 1945 – Austria

Commanders:

Gruppenführer Max Simon, 3.10.43 – 24.10.44
Brigadeführer Otto Baum, 24.10.44 – 8.5.45

17.SS-Panzergrenadier-Division Götz von Berlichingen

Formation name changes:

SS-Panzergrenadier-Division Götz von Berlichingen
17.SS-Panzergrenadier-Division Götz von Berlichingen

General Composition:

SS-Panzergrenadier-Regiment 37
SS-Panzergrenadier-Regiment 38
SS-Panzer-Abteilung 17
SS-Panzerjäger-Abteilung 17
SS-Sturmgeschütz-Abteilung 17
SS-Artillerie-Regiment 17
SS-Flak-Abteilung 17
SS-Nachrichten-Abteilung 17
SS-Panzer-Aufklärungs-Abteilung 17
SS-Pionier-Bataillon 17
SS-Divisions-Nachschubtruppen 17
SS-Panzer-Instandsetzungs-Abteilung 17
SS-Wirtschafts-Bataillon
SS-Sanitäts-Abteilung 17
SS-Feldpostamt 17
SS-Kriegsberichter-Zug 17
SS-Feldgendarmerie-Kompanie 17
SS-Feldersatz-Bataillon 17

Area of Operations:

June 1944 – Normandy
August 1944 – Champaign
October 1944 – Saarpfalz
April 1945 – Germany

Commanders:

Gruppenführer Werner Ostnedorff, 30.10.43 – ??.1.44
Oberführer Fritz Klingenberg, ??.1.44 – ??.??.44
Gruppenführer Werner Ostnedorff, ??.??.44 – 17.6.44
Standartenführer Otto Binge, 17.6.44 – 20.6.44
Brigadeführer Otto Baum, 20.6.44 – 1.8.44
Standartenführer Otto Binge, 1.8.44 – 30.8.44
Oberführer Dr. Eduard Deisenhofer, 30.8.44 – ??.9.44
Oberführer Thomas Müller,??.9.44 – ??.9.44
Standartenführer Gustav Mertsch, ??.9.44 – 21.10.44
Gruppenführer Werner Ostnedorff, 21.10.44 – 15.11.44
Standartenführer Hans Linger, 15.11.44 – 9.1.45
Oberst Gerhard Lindner, 9.1.45 – 21.1.45
Oberführer Fritz Klingenberg, 2.1.45 – 22.3.45
Standartenführer Jakob Fick, 22.3.45 – 26.3.45
Oberführer Georg Bochmann, 26.3.45 – 8.5.45

18.SS-Freiwilligen-Panzergrenadier-Division Horst Wessel

Formation name changes:

SS-Brigade (mot.)
1.SS-Brigade (mot.)

1.SS-Infanterie-Brigade (mot.)
18.SS-Freiwilligen-Panzergrenadier-Division Horst Wessel

Area of Operations:

August 1944 – Ukraine
November 1944 – Hungary
January 1945 – Slovakia
April 1945 – Silesia

Commanders:

Brigadeführer Wilhelm Trabant, 25.1.44 – 3.1.45
Gruppenführer Josef Fitzthum, 3.1.45 – 10.1.45
Oberführer Georg Bochmann, 10.1.45 – ??.3.45
Standartenführer Heinrich Petersen, ??.3.45 – 8.5.45

19. Waffen-Grenadier-Division der SS (Lett. Nr.2)

Formation name changes:

SS-Brigade (mot) 2
Lettische SS-Freiwilligen-Brigade
2. Lettische SS-Freiwilligen Brigade
19. Lettische SS-Freiwilligen-Division
19. Waffen-Grenadier-Division der SS (Lett. Nr.2)

Area of Operations:

April 1944 – Northern Front Russia
November 1944 – April 1945 – Courland

Commanders:

Oberführer Friedrich-Wilhelm Bock, 15.3.44 – 13.4.44
Gruppenführer Bruno Streckenbach, 13.4.44 – 8.5.45

20. Waffen-Grenadier-Division der SS (Estnische Nr. 1)

Formation name changes:

Estnische SS-Legion
Estnische SS-Freiwilligen-Brigade
3. Estnische SS-Freiwilligen Brigade
20. Estnische SS-Freiwilligen-Division
20. Waffen-Grenadier-Division der SS (Estnische Nr.1)

Area of Operations:

March/October 1944 – Estonia
February/April 1945 – Schlesien

Commanders:

Brigadeführer Franz Augsberger, 24.1.44 – 19.3.45
Brigadeführer Berthold Maack, 19.3.45–8.5.45

21. Waffen-Gebirgs-Division der SS Skanderbeg (Alban.Nr.1)

Formation name changes:

Waffen-Gebirgs-Division der SS Skanderbeg (Alban.Nr.1)
21.Waffen-Gebirgs-Division der SS Skanderbeg (Alban.Nr.1)

Area of Operations:

June/September 1944 – Albania
October/November 1944 – Yugoslavia
December 1944 – January 1945 – Croatia

Commanders:

Brigadeführer August Schmidt Huber, 1.5.44 – 20.1.45

22. SS-Freiwilligen-Kavallerie-Division Maria Theresia (ung.)

Area of Operations:

July 1944 – February 1945 – Hungary

Commanders:

Brigadeführer August Zehender, 21.4.44 – 11.2.45

23. SS-Freiwilligen-Panzergrenadier-Division Nederland

Formation name changes:

October 1943

48.SS-Freiwilligen-Panzergrenadier-Regiment General Seyffard
49.SS-Freiwilligen-Panzergrenadier-Regiment de Ruyter
23.SS-Artillerie-Regiment
23.SS-Panzerjäger-Abteilung
23.SS-Aufklärungs-Abteilung
23.SS-Pioneer-Abteilung
23.SS-Nachrichten-Abteilung
23.SS-Feldersatz-Bataillon
23.SS Divisional Support Units

May 1944

48.SS-Freiwilligen-Panzergrenadier-Regiment General Seyffard
49.SS-Freiwilligen-Panzergrenadier-Regiment de Ruyter
23.SS-Artillerie-Regiment
23.SS-Aufklärungs-Abteilung
23.SS-Panzerjäger-Abteilung
23.SS-Pioneer-Abteilung
23.SS-Nachrichten-Abteilung
23.SS-Feldersatz-Abteilung
23.SS Divisional Support Units

Area of Operations:

February/April 1945 – Pomerania

Commanders:

Brigadeführer Jürgen Wagner, 9.3.45 – 8.5.45

23. Waffen-Gebirgs-Division der SS Kama (kroat.Nr.2)

Formation name changes:

Waffen-Gebirgs-Division
23.SS-Gebirgs-Division
23.Waffen-Gebirgs-Division der SS Kama (kroat.Nr.2)

General Composition:

Waffen-Gebirgsjäger-Regiment der SS 55 (kroat.Nr.3)
Waffen-Gebirgsjäger-Regiment der SS 56 (kroat.Nr.4)
SS-Gebirgs-Artillerie-Regiment 23
SS-Aufklärungs-Abteilung 23
SS-Panzerjäger-Abteilung 23
SS-Flak-Abteilung 23
SS-Pionier-Bataillon 23
SS-Gebirgs-Nachrichten-Abteilung 23
SS-Gebirgs-Sanitäts-Abteilung
SS-Feldersatz-Battillon 23

Area of operation:

Balkans 1944

Commanders:

Standartenführer Helmuth Raithel 1.7.44 – 28.9.44
Brigadeführer Gustav Lombard 28.9.44 – 01.10.44

24. Waffen-Gebirgs – (Karstjäger) Division der SS

Formation name changes:

SS-Karstwehr-Kompanie
SS-Karstwehr-Abteilung
Waffen-Gebirgs (Karstjäger) Division der SS
24. Waffen-Gebirgs (Karstjäger) Division der SS

Area of Operation:

Used for anti-partisan duties in Istria from 9.44. Surrendered 5.45 at Isonzo to British forces.

Commanders:

Obersturmbannführer Karl Marx, ??.8.44 – 5.12.44
Sturmbannführer Werner Hahn, 5.12.44 – 10.2.45
Oberführer Adolf Wagner, 10.2.45 – 8.5.45

25. Waffen-Grenadier-Division der SS Hunyadi (ung.Nr.1)

Area of Operation:

January/April 1945 – Germany

Commanders:

Oberführer Thomas Müller, ??.11.44 – ??.11.44
Gruppenführer Josef Grassy,??.11.44 – 8.5.45

26. Waffen-Grenadier-Division der SS (ung.Nr.2)

Area of Operation:

March/April 1945 – Germany

Commanders:

Standtenführer Rolf Tiemann, ??.11.44 – ??.11.44
Oberführer Zoltan Pisky, ??.11.44 – 23.1.45
Oberführer Laszlo Deak, 23.1.45 – 29.1.45

Brigadeführer Berthold Maack, 29.1.45 – 21.3.45
Gruppenführer Jozef Grassy, 21.3.45 – 8.5.45

27. SS-Freiwilligen-Grenadier-Division Langemarck

Formation name changes:

SS-Freiwilligen Standarte Nordwest
SS-Freiwilligen Verband Flandern (Landesverband Flandern)
SS-Batallion Flandern
SS-Freiwilligen Legion Flandern
SS-Freiwilligen Sturmbrigade Langemarck
6. SS-Freiwilligen-Sturmbrigade Langemarck
27. SS-Freiwilligen-Grenadier-Division Langemarck

Area of Operations:

February/April 1945 – Pomerania

Commanders:

Obersturmbannführer Conrad Schellong, ??.9.44 – ??.10.44
Oberführer Thomas Müller, ??.10.44 – 2.5.45

28. SS-Freiwilligen-Panzergrenadier-Division Wallonien

Formation name changes:

Wallonische Legion
SS-Freiwilligen-Brigade Wallonien
SS-Sturmbrigade Wallonien
5. SS-Freiwilligen-Sturmbrigade Wallonien
SS-Freiwilligen-Grenadier-Division Wallonien
28. SS-Freiwilligen-Grenadier-Division Wallonien
28. SS-Freiwilligen-Panzergrenadier-Division Wallonien

Area of Operations:

February/April 1945 – Pomerania

Commanders:

Standtenführer Lucien Lippert 01.2.44 – 14.2.44
Oberführer Leon Degrelle 14.2.45 – 8.5.45

29. Waffen-Grenadier-Division der SS (Russische Nr. 1)

Area of Operation:

Planned formation August 1st 1944 in the Warsaw area from the Brigade Kaminski, but this was cancelled due to the unreliability of the troops. Brigade Kaminski was used to combat the uprising in Warsaw that raged during August 1944.

Commanders:

Brigadeführer Bronislav Kaminski, 17.6.44 – 19.8.44
Brigadeführer Christoph Diehm, 19.8.44 – ??.8.44

29. Waffen-Grenadier-Division der SS (Ital.Nr.1)

Formation name changes:

1.Italienische Freiwilligen-Sturm-Brigade Milizia Armata
1.Sturmbrigade Italienische Freiwilligen-Legion
Waffen-Grenadier-Brigade der SS (Italienische Nr.1)
29.Waffen-Grenadier-Division der SS (ital.Nr.1)

General Composition:

81.Waffen-Grenadier-Regiment der SS
82.Waffen-Grenadier-Regiment der SS
29.SS-Artillerie-Regiment
29.SS-Panzerjäger-Abteilung
29.SS-Fusilier-Battalion
29.SS-Nachrichten-Kompanie
29.SS-Pioneer-Kompanie
29th SS Divisional Support Units

Area of Operations:

March 1945 – Italy (Formed from Waffen-Grenadier-Brigade der SS (ital.Nr.1)

Commanders:

Brigadeführer Pietro Mannelli, ??.9.44 – ??.9.44
Brigadeführer Peter Hansen, ??.9.44 – ??.10.44
Brigadeführer Gustav Lombard, ??.10.44 – ??.11.44
Standtenführer Constantin Heldmann, ??.11.44 – ??.??.45
Oberführer Erwin Tzschoppe, ??.??.45 – 4.??.45

30. Waffen-Grenadier-Division der SS (Russische Nr.2)

Formation name changes:

Schutzmannschaft-Brigade Siegling
30.Waffen-Grenadier-Division der SS (Russische Nr.2)

General Composition:

75.Waffen-SS-Grenadier-Regiment
76.Waffen-SS-Grenadier-Regiment
77.Waffen-SS-Grenadier-Regiment
30.Waffen-SS-Artillerie-Regiment
30.SS-Aufklärungs-Abteilung
30.SS-Pioneer-Abteilung
30.SS-Nachrichten-Abteilung
30.SS-Feldersatz-Bataillon
30.SS Divisional Support Units

Area of Operations:

October 1944 – Belfort (Reserve)
December 1944 – Upper Rhine

Commanders:

Standtenführer Hans Siegling: 18.8.44 – 31.12.44

30. Waffen-Grenadier-Division der SS (Weißruthenische Nr.1)

Formation name changes:

Schutzmannschaft-Brigade Siegling
30.Waffen-Grenadier-Division der SS (Russische Nr.2)
Waffen-Grenadier-Brigade der SS (Weißruthenische)
30.Waffen-Grenadier-Division der SS (Weißruthenische Nr.1)

Area of Operation:

March/April 1945 – Grafenwöhr

Commanders:

Standtenführer Hans Siegling, 10.2.45 – ??.4.45

31. SS-Freiwilligen-Grenadier-Division

Area of Operations:

November 1944 – Hungary
February/May 1945 – Eastern Front/Germany

Commanders:

Brigadeführer Gustav Lombard, 1.10.44 – ??.4.45
Brigadeführer Wilhelm Trabandt, ??.4.45 – 8.5.45

32. SS-Freiwilligen-Grenadier-Division 30. Januar

General Composition:

86.SS-Freiwilligen-Grenadier-Regiment
87.SS-Freiwilligen-Grenadier-Regiment
88.SS-Freiwilligen-Grenadier-Regiment
32.SS-Freiwilligen-Artillerie-Regiment
32.Waffen-SS-Panzerjäger-Abteilung
32.Waffen-SS-Füsilier-Abteilung
32.Waffen-SS-Flak-Abteilung
32.Waffen-SS-Pioneer-Abteilung
32.Waffen-SS-Nachrichten-Abteilung
32.Waffen-SS-Feldersatz-Bataillon
32.SS Divisional Support Units

Area of Operations:

February/April 1945 – Frankfurt/Oder

Commanders:

Standtenführer Rudolf Mühlenkamp, 1.30.45 – 2.05.45
Standtenführer Joachim Richter, 2.05.45 – 2.17.45
Oberführer Adolf Ax, 2.17.45 – 3.15.45
Standtenführer Hans Kempin, 3.15.45 – 5.8.45

33. Waffen-Grenadier-Division der SS Charlemagne

Formation name changes:

Französische SS-Freiwilligen-Grenadier-Regiment
Französische SS-Freiwilligen-Sturmbrigade and
verst.Franz.Gren.Inf.Reg.638 (LVF)

Waffen-Grenadier-Brigade der SS Charlemagne (Französische Nr.1)
33.Waffen-Grenadier-Division der SS Charlemagne (Französische Nr.1)

General Composition:

SS-Waffen-Grenadier-Regiment 57
SS-Waffen-Grenadier-Regiment 58
33.SS-Artillerie-Bataillon
33.SS-Panzerjäger-Bataillon
33.SS-Pionier-Kompanie
33.SS-Nachrichten-Kompanie
33.SS-Feldersatz-Kompanie
33rd SS Divisional Support Units

Area of Operations:

February/March 1945 – Pomerania
April 1945 – Berlin

Commanders

Waffen Oberführer der SS Edgard Puaud
SS-Brigadeführer Dr. Gustav Krukenberg
SS-Standtenführer Walter Zimmermann

34.SS-Freiwilligen-Grenadier-Division Landstorm Nederland

Formation name changes:

SS-Grenadier-Regiment 1 Landwacht Niederlande
SS-Freiwilligen-Grenadier-Brigade Landstorm Nederland
34. SS-Freiwilligen-Grenadier-Division Landstorm Nederland

Area of Operations:

March/April 1945 – Holland

Commanders:

Brigadeführer Joachim Ziegler, ??.4.43 – 20.4.44
Brigadeführer Jürgen Wagner, 20.4.44 – 2.11.44
Oberführer Martin Kohlroser, 2.11.44 – 8.5.45

35.SS und Polizei-Grenadier-Division

General Composition:

89.SS und Polizei-Grenadier-Regiment
90.SS und Polizei-Grenadier-Regiment
91.SS und Polizei-Grenadier-Regiment
35.SS und Polizei-Artillerie-Regiment
35.SS und Polizei-Panzerjäger-Abteilung
35.SS und Polizei-Fusilier-Abteilung
35.SS und Polizei-Pioneer-Abteilung
35.SS und Polizei-Nachrichten-Abteilung
35th SS Supply and Support units

Area of Operations:

March 1945 – River Oder

Commanders:

Oberführer Johannes Wirth, ??.2.45 – 1.3.45
Standtenführer Rüdiger Pipkorn, 1.3.45 – 8.5.45

36.Waffen-Grenadier-Division der SS

Formation name changes:

Wilddiebkommando Oranienburg
Sonderkommando Dr. Dirlewanger
SS-Sonderbataillon Dirlewanger
SS-Regiment Dirlewanger
SS-Sonderregiment Dirlewanger
SS-Sturmbrigade Dirlewanger
36. Waffen-Grenadier-Division

General Composition:

72.Waffen-Grenadier-Regiment der SS
73.Waffen-Grenadier-Regiment der SS
??.Panzer-Abteilung
687.Pioneer-Brigade (Heer)
1244.Grenadier-Regiment
Parts of the 681.schwere-Panzerjager-Abteilung
various divisional support elements

Area of Operations:

April 1945 – Lausitz

Commanders:

Oberführer Dr. Oskar Dirlewanger, 5.3.45 – ??.5.45
Brigadeführer Fritz Schmedes, ??.5.45 – ??.5.45

37.SS-Freiwilligen-Kavallerie-Division

Area of Operations:

March/April 1945 – Hungary

Commanders:

Oberführer Waldemar Fegelein, 26.2.45 – ??.3.45
Standartenführer Karl Gesele, ??.3.45 – 8.5.45

38.SS-Grenadier-Division Nibelungen

Formation name changes:

SS-Junkerschule Bad Tölz
SS-Division Junkerschule
38.SS-Grenadier-Division Nibelungen

General Composition:

SS-Panzergrenadier-Regiment 95
SS-Panzergrenadier-Regiment 96
SS-Artillerie-Abteilung 38
SS-Panzerjäger-Abteilung 38
SS-Pioneer-Abteilung 38
SS-Ausbildung und Ersatz Abteilung 38
38th Divisional Support Units

Area of Operations:

April 1945 – Upper Bavaria
8 May 1945 – Surrendered to American Forces

Commanders:

Standtenführer Hans Kempin, 01.3.45 – 15.3.45
Obersturmbannführer Richard Schulz-Kossens, 06.4.45 – ??.4.45
Brigadeführer Heinz Lammerding, ??.4.45 – ??.4.45 (Assigned, but never posted)
Brigadeführer Karl Reichsritter von Oberkamp, ??.4.45 – ??.4.45 (Assigned, but never posted)
Gruppenführer Martin Stange, 4.??.45 – 5.08.45

APPENDIX II

Weapons and Equipment

The bulk of the weapons and equipment used by the *Waffen-SS* throughout the war was more or less identical to that used by the *Wehrmacht*. A number of small arms, particularly those of foreign origin, saw considerable use in the units of the *Waffen-SS* due to the *Wehrmacht's* reluctance to supply sufficient quantities of German-produced hardware to Himmler's elite force. The *Waffen-SS* used a huge variety of weaponry, everything from small arms to heavy tanks. The elite SS Panzer divisions, especially, were equipped with Germany's best tanks and supporting armoured vehicles. From 1943 onward, *Waffen-SS* troops were normally the first to be furnished with a host of new modern weaponry. However, even these elite troops were curtailed by never-ending shortages and were supplied with various weapons and equipment in order to sustain them on the battlefield long enough to drive back the growing enemy forces.

During the last two years of the war the *Waffen-SS* supplemented the finest hardware the German armaments industry could produce with many standard popular weapons and equipment used by their Wehrmacht counterparts. Below are the principle types of weaponry used by the *Waffen-SS,* especially during the last two years of the war.

Popular Waffen-SS Weapons and Equipment
Small Arms

Pistole 08 Pistol or Luger
Pisztoly 37M Hungarian Service Pistol
Frommer 7.65mm Hungarian Pistol
Model 1914 Norwegian Service Pistol
Fallschirmjäger 42 Automatic Rifle
Maschinenkarabiner 42
Gewehr 41 (W) Self-Loading Rifle
Maschinenpistole (MP) 28
Maschinenpistole (MP) 43
Sturmgewehr 44 (Assault Rifle)
Maschinenpistole (MP) 38
Maschinenpistole (MP) 40
Kar 98K Bolt-Action Rifle

Infantry Support Weapons

Maschinengewehr 34 (MG)
Maschinengewehr 42 (MG)
5cm Leichte Granatwerfer (leGW) 36 Mortar
15cm Nebelwerfer 41 (NbW 41)
21cm Nebelwerfer 42 (NbW 42)
Flammenwerfer (FIW) 41
Steilhandgrenate 39

Anti-tank and Anti-aircraft Weapons

7.92mm Panzerbüsche 38 Anti-Tank Rifle
7.92mm Panzerbüsche 39 Anti-Tank Rifle
3.7cm Pak 35/36 Anti-Tank Gun
5cm Pak 38 Anti-Tank Gun
7.5cm Pak 40 Heavy Anti-Tank Gun
8.8cm Pak 43 Heavy Anti-Tank Gun
Faustpatrone 30 Anti-Tank Rocket
Raketenpanzerbüsche (RPzB) 54 Anti-Tank Rocket Launcher
2cm Flugabwehrkanone (Flak) 30
2cm Flugabwehrkanone (Flak) 38
8.8cm Flugabwehrkanone (Flak) 18

Artillery

10.5cm leFH 18 Light Field Howitzer
7.5cm Leichte Feldkanone 18 (leFK)
7.5cm Feldkanone 40 (FK 40)
10cm Kanone 18 (s 10cm K 18)
15cm Schwere Feldhaubitze 18 (sFH 18)
21cm Mörser 18 (21cm Mrs 18) Heavy Gun

Armoured Cars and Halftracks
Armoured Cars

Sd.Kfz.221
Sd.Kfz.222
Sd.Kfz.223
Sd.Kfz.231
Sd.Kfz.234
Sd.Kfz.260
Sd.Kfz.261
Sd.Kfz.263

Artillery Prime Mover Halftracks

Sd.Kfz.2
Sd.Kfz.6
Sd.Kfz.7
Sd.Kfz.8
Sd.Kfz.9
Sd.Kfz.10
Sd.Kfz.11

Light Armoured Reconnaissance Halftracks

Sd.Kfz.250 Series (12 Variants)

Light Ammunition Carrier Halftrack

Sd.Kfz.252
Sd.Kfz.253

Medium Armoured Personnel Carrier Halftrack

Sd.Kfz.251 (22 Variants)

Panzers

Pz.Kpfw.III (Later Variants)
Pz.Kpfw.IV (Later Variants)
Pz.Kpfw.V Panther
Pz.Kpfw.VI. Tiger.I
Pz.Kpfw.VI. Tiger.II

Assault Guns and Tank Destroyers

Sturmgeschütz (StuG.III) (Later Variants)
Sturmgeschütz (StuG.IV)
Panzerjager Marder.I
Panzerjäger Marder.II
Panzerjäger Marder.III
Panzerjäger Nashorn
Panzerjäger Hummel
Panzerjäger Wespe
Jagdpanzer IV/70 Tank Destroyer
Jagdpanzer 38 (t) Hetzer
Jagdpanzer V Jagdpanther

APPENDIX III

Divisional Strength & Organisation Tables

12.SS.Panzer-Division *Hitlerjugend*

Table of Strength Report

Normandy Sector [1 June 1944]

Troop Strength	Official Strength	Shortages	Actual Total
Officers	664	144	520
NCOs	4,575	2,192	2,383
Other Ranks	15,277	2,360+	17,637
Hiwis	1,103	887	216
Total amount	20,516	24+	20,540

Total losses 1 May–1 June 1944

Troop Strength	Killed	Wounded	Missing
Officers	1	—	—
NCOs	10	6	—
Other Ranks	10	5	—
Total amount	21	11	—

Relacements to the front

Troop Strength	Replacements	Recovered
Officers	26	—
NCOs / Other Ranks	125 + 216 Hiwis	—

Over 1 year's non-leave

TOTAL	181
12–18 Months	170
19–24 Months	8
24 Months +	3

[Translated 12.SS Strength Report From Original Document]

4. Kurzes Werturteil des Kommandeurs:

1. <u>Ausbildungsstand:</u>

Die Division außer SS-Pz. Jäger-Abt.12 und SS-Nebelwerfer-Abt.12 befindet sich in der Verbandsausbildung.)

2. <u>Besondere Schwierigkeiten:</u>

a) Fehl von 3 Pz. Bef.-Wagen V,
b) Fehl an Bergepanzern,
c) Fehl der sollmäßigen Kfz.-Ausstattung der Panther-Abt.,
d) Der I.(Sf.)/SS-Pz. Art.Rgt.12 fehlen noch 2 Art. Beob.-Panzer (III)
e) Mangel an Mun.-Trägern für I.(Sf.)/SS-Pz. Art.Rgt.12,
f) Mangel an 1 t - Zugmaschinen zum Umbau der 2 cm Flak (mot-Z) in 2 cm Flak (Sf.),
g) Fehl von 12 Sd.-Kfz. 222 und 6 Sd.-Kfz. 233 bei SS-Pz.Aufkl.Abt
h) Fehl von 11 SPW bei SS-Pz. Nachr.-Abt. 12,
i) Fehl sämtlicher Zugmittel für SS-Werfer-Abt. 12,
k) Fehl der Befehlspanzer für SS-Pz. Jäger-Abt. 12.

3. <u>Einsatzbereitschaft:</u>

Die Division ist für Angriffsaufgaben einsatzbereit.

SS-Brigadeführer und
Generalmajor der Waffen-SS

<u>Anmerkung</u> zur "Personellen Lage":

58 Unterführer und Mannschaften sind seit 1.5., bzw. 15.5. zu den Junkerschulen kommandiert. Ihre Versetzung wurde bisher nicht verfügt.

5. Kurze Stellungnahme der vorgesetzten Dienststelle:

Division ist mit Ausnahme der Werferabteilung und der Panzer-Jäger-Abteilung im Westen für jede Aufgabe voll einsatzbereit.

Für das Generalkommando
Der Chef des Generalstabes

Original 12.SS.Pz.Div. Vehicle Shortage Report, dated: 1 June 1944

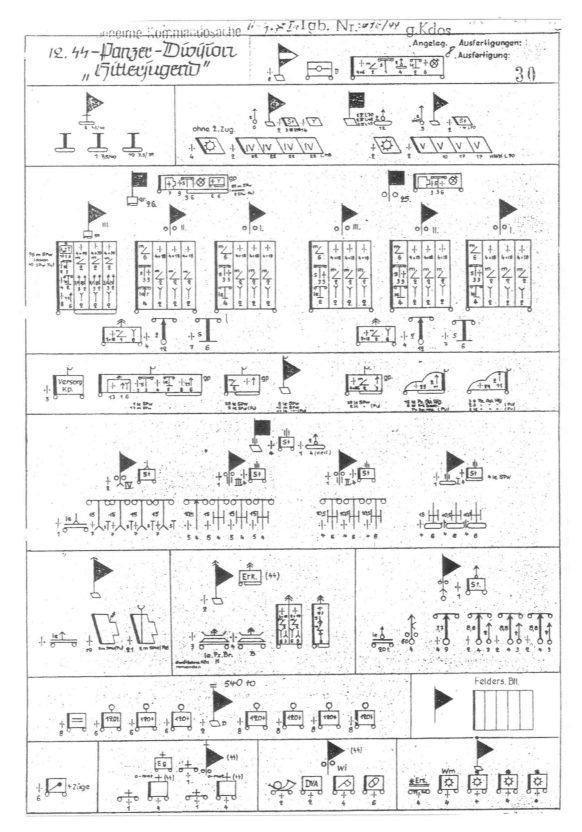

Original 12.SS.Pz.Div. Organisation Chart, dated: 1 June 1944

[The following shows the strength and organisation of a typical premier Waffen-SS division on the Western Front prior to the Normandy landings in early June 1944. The organisation of the SS Panzer division was transformed from the Type 43 model Panzer division into the Type 44 units used during the Normandy campaign. The reader will note that the manpower strength is considerably high following weeks of rest and refit, and this includes stocks of armoured and semi-tracked vehicles]

1.SS.Panzer-Division Leibstandarte *Adolf Hitler*

Strength Report [Normandy Sector 1 June 1944]

Division Stab

(Administration section, mapping unit, divisional security, and later to include military police company)
100% manpower
4 LMG

Div. Kartenstelle

100% manpower

Div. Begleitkompanie

100% manpower
8 LMG. 4 x 2cm Towed Flak Guns

SS.Panzer-Regiment.1

Regiment Stab

(With Signals, reconnaissance, engineer and flak units)
100% manpower
14 LMG

1.Panzer-Abteilung

(With signal, reconnaissance, engineer and flak units)
87.2% manpower
39 Pz.Kpfw.V Panther (4 Companies each of 17 tanks and workshop platoon)
31 LMG

2.Panzer-Abteilung

(With signal, reconnaissance, engineer and flak units)
100% manpower
50 Pz.Kpfw.IV (2 companies each of 22 Pz.Kpfw.IVs)
9 LMG

Pionier-Kompanie

81% manpower

1. Werkstatt-Kompanie

100% manpower

SS.Panzergrenadier-Regiment.1

Regiment Stab

90% manpower
3 x Towed 7.5cm Pak

1.Bataillon

96% manpower
3 LMG
5 HMG

14 x 81mm Mortars
4 x Towed 7.5cm Inf.Guns
1 x Towed 15cm Inf.Gun
2 x 7.5cm Towed Pak Guns

2.Bataillon

84% manpower
18 LMG
4 HMG
9 x 81mm Mortars
2 x Towed 7.5cm Pak Guns
4 x Towed 7.5cm Inf. Guns

3.Bataillon

86% manpower
15 LMG
3 HMG
9 x 81mm Mortars
3 x Towed 7.5cm Pak Guns
4 x Towed 7.5cm Inf.Guns

Flak Kompanie

94% manpower
12 x 2cm Flak Guns

Infanteriegeschütz Kompanie

94% manpower
3 LMG
(0 Heavy Weapons)

Panzerjäger Kompanie

70% manpower
(0 Heavy Weapons)

Pionier Kompanie

80% manpower
(0 Heavy Weapons)

SS.Panzergrenadier-Regiment.2

Regiment Stab

85% manpower
8 LMG
4 x 5cm Towed Pak guns
Medium Armoured Halftracks

1. Bataillon

94% manpower

32 LMG
10 x 81mm Mortars
4 x 7.5cm Towed Inf.Guns
1 x 15cm Inf. Gun
2 x 5cm Towed Pak Guns
2 x 7.5cm Towed Pak Guns

2.Bataillon

95% manpower
46 LMG
9 x 81cm Mortars
4 x 7.5cm Towed Inf.Guns
4 x 7.5cm Towed Pak Guns

3.Bataillon

90% manpower
17 LMG
6 x 81mm Mortars
4 x 7.5cm Towed Pak Guns
2 x 7.5cm Towed Inf.Guns

Flak Kompanie

100% manpower
12 x 2cm Towed Flak Guns

Infanteriegeschütz Kompanie

100% manpower
3 x 15cm SP Guns

Panzerjäger Kompanie

53% manpower
(0 Heavy Weapons)

SS.Aufklärungs-Abteilung

100% manpower
12 LMG

1.

Armoured Car Company
4 x Sd.Kfz.222 Armoured Car

2.

Armoured Car Company
12 LMG

3.

Armoured Reconnaissance Company
6 LMG
Light Armoured Halftracks

4.

Armoured Reconnaissance Company
6 LMG
Light Armoured Halftracks

5.

Heavy Company

Medium Armoured Halftracks
1 x 15cm Towed Inf.Gun
2 x 7.5cm Towed Inf.Guns
3 x 7.5cm Towed Pak Guns
1 x 2cm Towed Flak Guns

Versorgungs Kompanie

2 LMG

SS.Sturmgeschütz-Abteilung.1

100% manpower
14 LMG
45 Assault Guns

SS.Panzer-Artillerie-Regiment.1

Regiment Stab

100% manpower
4 LMG

1.Abteilung

80% manpower
19 LMG
18 x 105mm Towed LeFH 18 Guns

2.Abteilung

83% manpower
6 Wespe
6 Hummel

3.Abteilung

82% manpower
4 x 105mm Kanone
12 x 150mm SFH

4.Abteilung

88% manpower
10 x 15cm Nebelwerfer

SS.Flak-Abteilung

91% manpower
1 LMG
20 x 8.8cm Towed Flak Guns
2 x 3.7cm Towed Flak Guns
2 x 60cm Searchlights

SS.Panzer-Pionier-Bataillon

(With signal and armoured reconnaissance units. 2 motorised companies, 1 armoured company in medium armoured halftracks and up to 2 bridging columns)
62% manpower

1.Kompanie

10 LMG
4 HMG
4 x 81mm Mortars
Medium Halftracks

2.Kompanie

10 LMG

3.Kompanie

1 LMG

Brucken Kolonne

SS.Panzer-Nachrichten-Abteilung

(Had an HQ section and radio and telephone communications companies, each well-equipped with various armoured halftracks and softskin vehicles. The battalion also included a light supply column)
100% manpower
40 LMG

SS.Nachschubtruppen

(This formed the complete basis of all the divisional logistics and comprised of a HQ section, 6–8 trucked transport companies (each of 60 – 120 tonne capacity), and 1 workshop)
79% manpower
11 LMG
2 x Supply Companies
8 x Transport Companies

SS.Instadsetzungs-Abteilung.1

(With an HQ section, 3 or 4 motorised repair companies and a replacement parts company)
100% manpower
16 LMG

1 Supply Company
4 Workshop Repair Companies

SS.Wirtschaft-Bataillon.1

(With a HQ section)
100% manpower
11 LMG
1 Bakery Company
1 Butcher Company
1 Field Post Office
1 Administration Company

SS.Sanitäts-Abteilung

(With a HQ section)
75% manpower
8 LMG
2 Medical Companies
3 Ambulance Columns
1 Field Hospital

SS.Feldgendarmerie-Kompanie

(Comprised usually of 5 platoons in strength. In 1943 it was part of the divisional supply troops but by 1944 it moved to the divisional HQ section during the 'Type 44' reorganisation)
60% manpower
2 LMG

SS.Kriegsberichter.Zug.1

(Consisted of the divisional war correspondence unit)

APPENDIX IV

German Forces on the Western Front January 1945

Wehrmacht.Befh Denmark

166.Reserve-Division
160.Reserve-Division
233.Reserve.Panzer-Division
2.Gebirgsjäger-Div [Refitting]
6. Infanterie-Division

Western Front Reserves

Division-Stab z.b.V.604 (Stationed in the Netherlands)
70.Infanterie.Division

HEERSGRUPPE H

25.ARMEE

30.Korps
346.Infanterie-Division

88.Armee-Korps

711.Infanterie-Division
6.Fallschirmjäger-Division
2.Fallschirmjäger-Division

1. FALLSCHIRMJÄGER-ARMEE

7.Fallschirmjäger-Division
2. Fallschirmjäger-Korps
606.Division

86. Armee-Korps

84.Infanterie-Division
180.Infanterie-Division
190.Infanterie-Division

HEERESGRUPPE B

15.ARMEE

10.SS.Panzer.Division Frundsberg

12.SS-Korps

176.Infanterie-Division
59.Infanterie-Division
183. Volksgrenadier-Division

81.Armeekorps

47.Volksgrenadier-Division

353.Infanterie-Division
363. Volksgrenadier-Division

74.Armeekorps

85.Infanterie-Division
272. Volksgrenadier-Division
326. Volksgrenadier-Division

67.Armeekorps

277.Volksgrenadier-Division
246.Volksgrenadier-Division
89. Infanterie-Division
3.Fallschirmjäger-Division

6.PANZER-ARMEE

12.Volksgrenadier-Division
66.Armee-Korps
18.Volksgrenadier-Division
62. Volksgrenadier-Division

II.SS.Panzer-Korps

9.SS.Panzer-Division Hohenstaufen
560.Volksgrenadier-Division
2.SS.Panzer.Division Das Reich

5.PANZER-ARMEE

I.SS.Panzer-Korps

340.Volksgrenadier-Division
12.SS.Panzer-Division Hitlerjugend

58.Panzer-Korps

116.Panzer-Division
9.Panzer-Division
2.Panzer-Division

39.Panzer-Korps

3.Panzergrenadier-Division
26.Volksgrenadier-Division
1.SS.Panzer-Division LAH

47.Panzer-Korps

Panzer-Division Lehr
Führer-Begleit-Division
15.Panzergrenadier-Division

7.ARMEE

11.Panzer-Division
85.Armee-Korps
352.Volksgrenadier-Division
79.Volksgrenadier-Division

80.Armee-Korps

276.Volksgrenadier-Division
212.Volksgrenadier-Division

53.Armee-Korps

5.Fallschirmjäger-Division
Führer-Grenadier-Division
9.Volksgrenadier-Divison

HEERESGRUPPE G

553.Volksgrenadier-Division

1.ARMEE

559.Volksgrenadier-Division
36.Volksgrenadier-Division
17.SS.Panzergrenadier-Division Götz von Berlichingen
25.Panzergrenadier-Division
21.Panzer-Division

13.SS-Korps

347.Infanterie-Division
19.Volksgrenadier-Division

80.Armee-korps

257.Volksgrenadier-Divison

Group Hoehne 89.Armee.Korps

361.Volksgrenadier-Division
245.Infanterie-Division
256.Volksgrenaider-Division

Marine-Oberkommando West

25.Armee-Korps
265.Infanterie-Division
319.Infanterie-Division
226.Infanterie-Division

Fest Lorient

14.SS.Korps
18.SS.Korps
716. Infanterie-Division

19.ARMEE

64.Armee.Korps

708.Volksgrenadier-Division + 716.Infanterie-Division
198.Infanterie-Division
189.Infanterie-Division
16. Volksgrenadier-Division

63.Armee-Korps

159.Infanterie-Division
269.Infanterie-Division
338.Infanterie-Division

RESERVES

23.Infanterie-Division
275.Volksgrenadier-Division
83.Infanterie-Division
182.ReserveDivision
48. Volksgrenadier-Division
167.Volksgrenadier-Division
182.Reserve.Division

German Forces on the Eastern Front January 1945

Heeresgruppe Nord

18. ARMEE

I. Armee-Korps

563.Volksgrenadier-Division
225.Infanterie-Division
32. Infanterie-Division
218.Infanterie-Division
11.Infanterie-Division

III.SS.Panzer-Korps

4.SS.Panzergrenadier-Brigade Nederland
11.SS.Panzergrenadier-Division. Nordland
121.Infanterie-Division
10.Armee-Korps
132.Infanterie-Division
87.Infanterie-Division
30.Infanterie-Division

2.Armee-Korps

14. Panzer-Division
31.Volksgrenadier-Division
263.Infanterie-Division
126.InfanterieDivision

16.ARMEE

38. Armee-Korps

329.Infanterie-Division
205.Infanterie-Division
215.Infanterie-Division

50.Armee-Korps

389.Infanterie-Division
290.Infanterie-Division
122.Infanterie-Division
24.Infanterie-Division

VI.SS-Korps

93.Infanterie-Division
19.SS.Division Latvian 2
12.Luftwaffe-Feld-Division
4.Panzer-Division
12.Panzer.Division

227.Infanterie-Division

16.Armee-Korps

281.Infanterie-Division
81.Infanterie-Division

Heeresgruppe Mitte

7.Panzer-Division
18.Panzergrenadier-Division

Group Hauer

20.Panzer-Division

2.ARMEE

20.Armee-Korps

14.Infanterie-Division
292.Infanterie-Division
102.Infanterie-Division

23.Armee-Korps

5.Jäger-Division
7.Infanterie-Division
299.Infanterie-Division
129.Infanterie-Division

27.Armeekorps

542.Volksgrenadier-Division
252.Infanterie-Division
35.Infanterie-Division

4. ARMEE

5.Panzer-Division

55.Armee-Korps

547.Volksgrenadier-Division
562.Volksgrenadier-Division
203.Infanterie-Division

6.Armee-Korps

541.Volksgrenadier-Division

Group Hannibal

131.Infanterie-Division
558.Volksgrenadier-Division

41.Panzer-Korps

170.Infanterie-Division
367.Infanterie-Division
50.Infanterie-Division
28.Jäger-Division
21.Infanterie-Division
61.Infanterie-Division

3.PANZER-ARMEE

26.Armee-Korps

549.Volksgrenadier-Division
349.Volksgrenadier-Division
1.Infanterie-Division
69.Infanterie-Division

9.Armee-Korps

56.Infanterie-Division
561.Volksgrenadier-Division
548.Volksgrenadier-Division
551.Volksgrenadier-Division

28.Armee-Korps

58.Infanterie-Division
95.Infanterie-Division

Heeresgruppe A

24.Panzer-Korps
40.Panzer-Korps
344.Infanterie-Division
16.Panzer-Division
17.Panzer-Division
20.Panzergrenadier-Division
19.Panzer-Division
25.Panzer-Division
10.Panzergrenadier-Division

ARMEEGRUPPE HEINRICI

1. (HUNGARIAN) ARMEE

17.Armee-Korps

208.Infanterie-Division
3.Gebirgsjäger-Division
4.Gebirgsjäger-Division
24.Hungarian-Infanterie-Division
16.Hungarian-Infanterie-Division

1.PANZER-ARMEE

49.Gebirgs-Korps

1.Ski-Jäger-Division
97.Jäger-Division
254.Infanterie-Division
101.Jäger-Division

11.Armee-Korps

75.Infanterie-Division

100.Jager-Division
253.Infanterie-Division

17.ARMEE

XI.SS.Korps

545.Volksgrenadier-Division
78.Volksgrenadier-Division
320.Volksgrenadier-Division

59.Armee-Korps

544.Volksgrenadier-Division
359.Infanterie-Division
371.Infanterie-Division

4.PANZER-ARMEE

48.Panzer-Korps

304.Infanterie-Division
68.Infanterie-Division
168.Infanterie-Division

42.Armee-Korps

291.Infanterie-Division
88.Infanterie-Division
72.Infanterie-Division
342.Infanterie-Division

9.ARMEE

56.Panzer-Korps

214.Infanterie-Division
17.Infanterie-Division

8.Armee-Korps

45.Volksgrenadier-Division
6.Volksgrenadier-Division
251.Infanterie-Division

46.Panzer-Korps

337.Volksgrenadier-Division
73.Infanterie-Division
Fest Warsaw

Heeresgruppe Sud

IV.SS-Panzer-Korps

3.SS.Panzer-Division Totenkopf
5.SS.Panzer-Division Wiking
711.Infanterie-Division
118.Jäger-Division
211.Infanterie-Division
96.Infanterie-Division

2.PANZER-ARMEE

68.Armee-Korps

44.Infanterie-Division

13.SS.Gebirgsjäger-Division Croatian Nr.1
71.Infanterie-Division

22.Gebirgs-Korps

1.Gebirgs-Division
3.Kavallerie-Brigade

ARMEEGRUPPE BALCK

3.HUNGARIAN.ARMY

2.Hungarian-Korps

25.Hungarian-Infanterie-Division

6.ARMEE

3.Panzer-Korps

1.Panzer-Division
23.Panzer-Division
4.Kavallerie-Brigade

Group Pape

3.Panzer-Division
1.Hungarian Kavallerie-Division
8.Panzer-Division
6.Panzer-Division
271.Volksgrenadier-Division

Group Kirchner (57.Panzerkorps)

72.Armee-Korps

6.Panzer-Division

2.Hungarian-Armoured-Division
3.Panzer-Division

57.Panzer-Korps

8.Panzer-Division
357.Infanterie-Division

IX.SS.Gebirgs-Korps

13.Panzer-Division + 10.Hungarian.Infanterie-Division
22.SS.Kavallerie-Division + 1.Hungarian.Armoured-Division
8.SS.Kavallerie-Division Florian Geyer
12.Hungarian-Reserve-Division
23.Hungarian-Infanterie-Division

8.ARMEE

9.Hungarian-Border-Division
27. Hungarian- Light-Division

9.Hungarian-Korps

29.Armee-Korps

8.Jäger-Division
15.Infanterie-Division
76.Infanterie-Division

4.Panzer-Korps

24.Panzer-Division
4.SS.Panzergrenadier-Division Polizei+ 18.SS.Panzergrenadier-Division
46.Infanterie-Division

APPENDIX VI

Combat Uniforms of the Waffen-SS 1943–45

General Notes

This section is not intended to provide a definite reference to the combat uniforms worn by all the *Waffen-SS* divisions that saw active service during the later half of the war, but simply to supply the reader with the general uniforms seen on the battlefront between 1943–45.

Tunics

The Waffen-SS service uniforms worn between 1943–45 were generally based on the typical Army-pattern M1940 tunic. They were field-grey in colour and manufactured from wool/rayon mixed material. The tunic had four box-pleated patch pockets. The collar patches displayed the typical wartime machine-embroidered runes or insignia of the attached division. The shoulder straps were piped in a number of various colours depending on rank. On the left sleeve was the standard machine-embroidered eagle and chevron displaying the rank. The most prominent piece of insignia was the cuff title worn by all premier *SS* formations. The lesser divisions, or those better known as non-German volunteer *SS* divisions wore tunics that varied considerably in quality. The design of the tunic was almost universal, but the volunteers, presumably to retain the individual soldier's national pride, normally wore the divisional emblem patch on the right collar, plus the national arm shield and the cuff title.

Camouflage Smocks and Uniforms

The *Waffen-SS* were the first soldiers in the world to be issued with camouflage clothing on a large scale. These camouflage printed uniforms became as much the hallmark of the *Waffen-SS* as the runes worn on their collars. The patterns, however, were quite varied and as a consequence a multitude of camouflage patterns were developed through the war. The camouflage jacket or smock was a very popular piece of uniform and was supposed to be worn over the wool service uniform and the field equipment. This loose fitting reversible smock was made from a high quality water-repellent cotton duck material, one side usually screen-printed in spring/summer colour scheme and the reverse showing autumn/winter colours. From 1943 onwards the camouflage patterns varied considerably, from the early type 1940 oakleaf camouflage smock, the M1942 second type oakleaf and palm tree camouflage smocks, M1943 pea pattern drill camouflage uniform, to the M1944 pea pattern camouflage drill uniform. It was not uncommon to see *Waffen-SS* soldiers in 1943–45, wearing a combination of the M1943 drill and M1944 herringbone twill camouflage uniforms. The difference in colours was quite apparent between the predominately ochre yellow 1943 jacket or trousers and the pinkish brown hue of the 1944 trousers or jacket.

Another item of camouflage clothing worn by the *Waffen-SS* during the war was the M1937 style camouflage tunic. It was made of herringbone twill, printed with pea pattern camouflage and resembled the classic M37 tunic, since it had pleated breast pockets with flaps lined with artificial silk.

In 1944, the camouflage blouse was introduced. This waist length blouse roughly resembled the M1944 *feldbluse* or the British battledress blouse in cut, though with open patch pockets. It was made from *Zeltbahn* material, with autumn colours on the outside, but was not reversible.

Winter Uniforms

The most universal item of winter clothing worn by the *Waffen-SS* was the two-piece snowsuit. This shapeless two-piece snowsuit consisting of a white jacket and white trousers was commonly worn by the SS, especially the volunteer combat formations. Another form of white snow camouflage clothing was the long overall coat, which buttoned right down the front of the garment. Large and shapeless, it was worn without a belt over any uniform and all the equipment. However, the snowsuit tended to restrict the wearer's freedom of movement and was not very popular by late 1943.

One of the most popular items of clothing in the winter was the reversible padded winter uniform, which was worn by both the *Wehrmacht* and *Waffen-SS* in the later war years. This padded grey/white suit was produced in the winter of 1942 43, and was the first truly reversible cold weather uniform offering both concealment and extra warmth to become available to the troops on the Eastern Front in large numbers. Originally the suit was in grey-green, although the *SS* had them produced in a darker steel-grey colour.

Another garment worn by the *SS* in the later war period was the Italian fur-lined, padded over-jacket, which was made from captured Italian camouflage material in 1944. The jacket was made large enough to be worn over the field equipment, so that a soldier's weapons and ammunition could also be kept warm in the extreme arctic conditions. In the cold weather the hood could be easily tightened around the head and helmet.

Panzer Uniform

The most common armoured uniform worn by the Panzers units of the *Waffen-SS* was the special black armoured crew uniform. The SS Panzer uniform varied from that of the Army version, and consisted of small and more rounded lapels and it lacked the pink upper lapel piping initially worn by all Army ranks. The black uniform was a very practical garment for all types of duty and was still seen in 1943 when the camouflage clothing specifically for armoured crews was introduced.

The armoured crews' camouflage overalls were designed entirely for concealment when the crewman was away from his vehicle. The overall was reversible with autumn browns inside, and a green oakleaf-type pattern for the spring and summer.

Another popular variation of the armoured uniform was the reed-green two-piece garment. However, by January 1944, it was decided to replace it with a two-piece printed pea pattern camouflage version. There were three slightly different models manufactured, but the cut did not vary.

Assault Gun Uniform

When designing the uniform for crews of tank destroyers and self-propelled assault guns serving in the Panzer and Panzergrenadier divisions, the Germans decided on using the same style and practical cut of the black Panzer uniform to produce a new version, known as the self-propelled gun crew uniform. This special uniform was made entirely of field-grey cloth with all the details of cut and design as those of the black Panzer uniform. However, the uniform did differ in respect to the *SS* collar insignia.

Another variation of the assault gun uniform, but introduced in the later part of the war was the pea style herringbone camouflage jacket with pointed lapels.

Steel Helmet

The most distinctive universal headgear issued to the *Waffen-SS* was the steel helmet. In particular during the second half of the war the *SS* wore three major models, the basic M1935 and M1940 to and the final M1942 pattern. By 1943 most of the steel helmets were predominantly covered with camouflage cloth that was held on by an envelope of material that slipped over the peak, and by three small sprung clips, one either side and one at the rear. The fabric, normally matching the camouflage smock, was printed on both sides in contrasting seasonal colour schemes for spring/summer and autumn/winter. However, even by 1943 there were still *Waffen-SS* soldiers, including those in the premier *SS* divisions that wore the single decal steel helmets without the camouflage fabric covering. The helmets had their previous shiny surface removed by soldiers daubing them with mud and camouflaging them with anything available, from vehicle paint to winter whitewash. In fact, by 1943 some artistic *SS* troops begun to mimic the various dot camouflage uniform patterns by applying paint to the helmet while covering it with chicken wire netting. The colours varied, but on many examples soldiers applied browns, greens and ochres, colours that were specifically issued to camouflage vehicles from mid-1943 onwards.

Bibliography & Notes

Part I

1. Operation Zitadelle

Notes

1.Kursk Order of Battle July 1943
Militärarchiv Freiburg/ Kursk/RHN68/K 9
2. 1.SS.Leibstandarte History Diary
Militärarchiv Freiburg/LAH/RH 19VMN

Documents

Ost-Dokumentation. 10 Nr.Opr. XI. C/4
Bundesarchiv Koblenz
Documents relating to the battle of Kursk were obtained through the Bundesarchiv Koblenz and the
    Militärarchiv in Freiburg.
Miscellaneous SS Records: Einwandererzentralstelle, Waffen-SS, and SS Oberabschnitte. National Archives,
    Microcopy T–354
Records of Headquarters, German High Command: National Archives, Microcopy T–81.

Published Material

Bundesverband der Soldaten der ehem Regts Kameradschaft. *Das Regiment D 1934 – 1945*
Heinrici, Gotthard: Zitadelle. *Wehrwissenschaftliche Rundschau*, 15
Tessin, G. *Verbaende und Truppen der deutsch. Wehrmacht und Waffen-SS, 1939 – 1945*

2. Kharkov and Beyond

Notes

1.Feldmarschall von Manstein's commendation
Various SS Records: Einwandererzentralstelle, Waffen-SS, and SS-Oberabschnitte. Washington: National
    Archives Section, Microcopy Roll T–354 [SS/T–354

Documents

Oberkommando der Wehrmacht (OKW). Washington: National Archives Section, Microcopy Roll T–77
    [OKW/T–77]
Reichsführer-SS und Chef der Deutsches Polizei). Washington: National Archives Section, Microcopy Roll T–
    175 [RFSS/T–175
Records of the Reich Leader of the SS and Chief of the German Police (Reichsführer-SS und Chef der
    Deutschen Polizei). National Archives, Microcopy T–175.

Published Material

Anon. *Aufbruch: Briefe von germanischen Freiwilligen der SS-Division Wiking*. Berlin Nibelungen Verlag. 1943
Hausser, Paul, *Waffen-SS im Einsatz*, Plesse Verlag, Gottingen, 1953.

3. Fighting Withdrawal

This chapter was researched mainly from the magazine of the Waffen-SS, *Der Freiwillige*, and post-battle reports obtained through Bundesarchiv Koblenz (Waffen-SS Ost-Dokmentation/3421.Vol.1.2.3.4. (12.Nr. Opr.XX D/5)

Documents

Various SS Records: Einwandererzentralstelle, Waffen-SS, and SS-Oberabschnitte. Washington: National Archives Section, Microcopy Roll T–354 [SS/T–354

Published Material

Anon. *Aufbruch: Briefe von germanischen Freiwilligen der SS-Division Wiking.* Berlin: Nibelungen Verlag, 1943
Kanis, K. *Waffen-SS im bild.* Gottingen: Plesse Verlag, 1957
Kratschmer, Ernst-Gunther, *Die Ritterkreuzträger der Waffen-SS.* Gottingen: Plesse Verlag, 1955

Part II

4. Southern Front

This chapter was researched mainly from the magazine of the Waffen-SS, *Der Freiwillige*, and post-battle reports obtained through Bundesarchiv Koblenz (Waffen-SS Ost-Dokmentation/3421.Vol.1.2.3.4. (12.Nr. Opr.XX D/5). The following also includes research through scattered documents of Heeresgruppe Süd found at Bundesarchiv Koblenz.

Notes

1. Wiking Diary
Anon. *Aufbruch: Briefe von germanischen Freiwilligen der SS-Division der SS-Division Wiking.* Berlin: Nibelungen Verlag, 1943.

Documents

Bundesarchiv Koblenz: Akten des Reichsführer-SS und chef der Deutschen Polizei, Personlicher Stab (NS/19.
Bundesarchiv Militärarchiv, Freiburg: Bestand Generalkommando SS Panzer-Korps (RS 2–2/1 BIS 31) – Splitterkaten der 3. SS-Panzer-Division Totenkopf, 1939 – 1945 (III.SS)
National Archives Microcopy T312, Records of German Field Commands, Armies: Armeeoberkommando 8 (Reels 54, 64, 66).

Published Material

Georg, Enno. *Die wirtschaftlichen Unternehmungen der SS.* (Schriftenreihe der Vierteljahrshefte fur Zeitgeschichte, No.7) Stuttgart: Deutsche Verlag-Anstalt, 1963.
Neufeldt, Hans-Joachim, Jurgen Huck, and Georg Tessin. *Zur Geschichte der Ordnungspolizei 1936 – 1945.* (Schriften des Bundesarchiv, Vol.3.) Koblenz: Bundesarchiv, 1957

5. Northern Front

This chapter was researched mainly from the magazine of the Waffen-SS, *Der Freiwillige*, and post-battle reports obtained through Bundesarchiv Koblenz (Waffen-SS Ost-Dokmentation/3421.Vol.1.2.3.4. (12.Nr. Opr.XX D/5)

Documents

National Archives: Microcopy T–313, Records of German Field Commands, Panzer Armies and Waffen-SS.
National Archives: Microcopy 314, Records of Waffen-SS/Wehrmacht Armee-Korps, Field commands and II.Armee-Korps (Reels 131, 132, 133)
Bundesarchiv Militärarchiv: SS-Panzer-Divisions (III/SS)

Published Material

Anon. *Die Wehrmacht im Kampf* (Series) No.3, No.4, No.7, No.8, No.11, No.14, No.15, No.20.
Kanis, K. *Waffen-SS im bild.* Gottingen: Plesse Verlag, 1957
Kratschmer, Ernst-Gunther, *Die Ritterkreuzträger der Waffen-SS.* Gottingen: Plesse Verlag, 1955

Newspaper Periodical

Bundesarchiv Koblenz: *Das Schwarze Korps, 1936 – 1945* (Official newspaper of the SS)

Part III

6. Normandy Campaign

This chapter was researched mainly from the magazine of the Waffen-SS, *Der Freiwillige*, and post-battle reports obtained through Bundesarchiv Koblenz (Waffen-SS Ost-Dokmentation/3421.Vol.1.2.3.4. (12.Nr. Opr.XX D/5)

Notes

1.SS-Sturmann Jochen Leykauff Diary: Hubert Meyer 12.SS.HJ Division
Best, Walter. *Mit der Leibstandarte im Westen eines SS-Kriegsberichter.* Munich: F.Eher, 1944
Diary of Meyer, Kurt (Panzermeyer). *Grenadiere.* Munich: Schild Verlag, 1957

Documents

War Diary Supreme Commander West: F/M, RH19 IV/84 D, Ia, No.10697/44)
Normandy Campaign Dokumentation Order of Battle and Divisional Strength of Waffen-SS Divisions:
    Bundesarchiv Militärarchiv Freiburg: Dokumentation RH10, RH20, RH24, RS3, MSGZ.
Battles of the Hitlerjugend: Consisted of reports and various documents from the War Diary Supreme
    Command West, appendices, orders, reports. Fuhrer Oder National Archives Microfilm T–175, roll 108.
Documents of the Order by the SS-Führerungshauptampt, command office of the Waffen-SS, organization diary
    No.784/43.

Published Material

Weidinger, Otto: *Das Reich Division*, Volume V

7. Watch on the Rhine

This chapter was researched mainly from the magazine of the Waffen-SS, *Der Freiwillige*, and post-battle reports obtained through Bundesarchiv Koblenz (Waffen-SS Ost-Dokmentation/3421.Vol.1.2.3.4. (12.Nr. Opr.XX D/5)

Documents

Hitlerjugend in the Ardennes: Appendix 17 General der Panzertruppen West, Ia No. 1775/44 regarding condition of HJ prior to combat.
Planning of the Ardennes: (BA-MA RHIV 1247)
German manpower and material allocations (BA-MA RH 19IV 76) This document includes the Ardennes Order
    of Battle for 15 December 1944.
Artillery Report Listings, strengths by Armee Korps, and divisions December 1944. US NARA Microfilm T311,
    18, 7021051–4
Miscellaneous SS Records: Einwandererzentralstelle, Waffen-SS, and SS Oberabschnitte. National Archives,
    Microcopy T–354
Oberkommando der Wehrmacht (OKW). Washington: National Archives Section, Microcopy Roll T–77
    [OKW/T–77]

Published Material

Bundesverband der Soldaten der ehem Regts Kameradschaft. *Das Regiment D 1934 – 1945*
Kanis, K. *Waffen-SS im bild.* Gottingen: Plesse Verlag, 1957
Kratschmer, Ernst-Gunther, *Die Ritterkreuzträger der Waffen-SS.* Gottingen: Plesse Verlag, 1955
Tessin, G. *Verbaende und Truppen der deutsch. Wehrmacht und Waffen-SS, 1939 – 1945*
Tiemann, R. *Der Malmedyprozess.* Osnabruck. 1990.

Part IV

8. Defending Poland

This chapter was researched mainly from the magazine of the Waffen-SS, *Der Freiwillige*, and post-battle reports obtained through Bundesarchiv Koblenz (Waffen-SS Ost-Dokmentation/3421.Vol.1.2.3.4. (12.Nr. Opr.XX D/5)

Documents

Various SS Records: Einwandererzentralstelle, Waffen-SS, and SS-Oberabschnitte. Washington: National Archives Section, Microcopy Roll T–354 [SS/T–354

Records of Headquarters, German Army High Command. National Archives, Microcopy T–81. Battle Report Strengths and Orders: Bundesarchiv Koblenz. BA-K121 A/L.1

Published Material

Degrelle, Leon: *Die verlorene Legion*. Stuttgart: Veritas Verlag. 1952.

9. Hungary

This chapter was researched mainly from the War Diary of Heeresgruppe Süd: National Archives. AOK 8 / RH19 V/69 and from the magazine of the Waffen-SS, *Der Freiwillige*, and post-battle reports obtained through Bundesarchiv Koblenz (Waffen-SS Ost-Dokmentation/3421.Vol.1.2.3.4. (12.Nr. Opr.XX D/5).

Documents

Documents of the Order by the SS-Führerungshauptampt, command office of the Waffen-SS, organization diary No.784/43.

Published Material

Anon. *Die Wehrmacht im Kampf* (Series) No.3, No.4, No.7, No.8, No.11, No.14, No.15, No.20.

Klietmann, *Die Waffen-SS. Eine Dokumentation,* Verlag Der Freiwillige, Osnabrück, 1965

Scheibert, H. *Panzergrenadier Division GD*. Utting, Dörfler, 1970

10. Final Battles

Notes

1. Deserters Sign: Taken from eye witness account from *SS-Sturmmann* Hurbert Redulic (München) to author interview April 1992

2. Latvian Volunteer Diary: Taken from typed letter from diarist Bartek Zborski to author interview June 1992

Documents

Bundesarchiv Militärarchiv, Freiburg: Bestand Generalkommando SS Panzer-Korps (RS 2–2/1 BIS 31) – Splitterkaten der 3. SS-Panzer-Division Totenkopf, 1939 – 1945 (III.SS)

National Archives Microcopy T312, Records of German Field Commands, Armies: Armeeoberkommando 8 (Reels 54, 64, 66).

Published Material

Anon. *Die Kämpfe um die Befreiung der Lausitz: wahrend der grossen Schlacht um Berlin, 1945*. VEB Domowina Verlag, 1975

Anon. *Die Wehrmacht im Kampf* (Series) No.3, No.4, No.7, No.8, No.11, No.14, No.15, No.20.

Kanis, K. *Waffen-SS im bild*. Gottingen: Plesse Verlag, 1957

Kratschmer, Ernst-Gunther, *Die Ritterkreuzträger der Waffen-SS*. Gottingen: Plesse Verlag, 1955

Neufeldt, Hans-Joachim, Jurgen Huck, and Georg Tessin. *Zur Geschichte der Ordnungspolizei 1936 – 1945*. (Schriften des Bundesarchiv, Vol.3.) Koblenz: Bundesarchiv, 1957

Schmidt-Richberg, *Der Endkampf auf dem Balkan*. 1955

Schultz-Naumann, Joachim, *The Last 30 Days: War Diary of the German Armed Forces High Command April to May 1945: The Battle For Berlin*, Madison Books, 1991

Steiner, Felix. *Die Freiwilligen: Idee and Opfergang*. Gottinggen: Plesse Verlag, 1958

Tiemann, R. *Der Malmedyprozess*. Osnabruck. 1990.

Newspaper Periodical

Bundesarchiv Koblenz: *Das Schwarze Korps, 1936 – 1945* (Official newspaper of the SS)

Also available from Helion & Company

For Europe
The French Volunteers of the Waffen-SS
Robert Forbes
528pp., circa 6 maps, 7 photos
Hardback   ISBN 1-874622-68-X

To the Bitter End
The Final Battles of Army Groups North Ukraine,
A, Centre, Eastern Front 1944–45
Rolf Hinze
232pp., c 30 b/w photos, 30 maps
Hardback   ISBN 1-874622-36-1

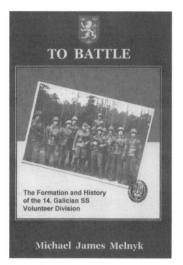

To Battle
The Formation and History of the 14th Waffen-SS
Grenadier Division
Michael Melnyk
400pp., 300+ b/w photos, illustrations, documents, maps
Paperback   ISBN 1-874622-19-1

A SELECTION OF FORTHCOMING TITLES

Panzer Lehr Division 1944–45 (Helion WWII German Military Studies volume 1)
edited by Fred Steinhardt   ISBN 1-874622-28-0

Under Himmler's Command: The Personal Recollections of Oberst Hans-Georg Eismann,
Operations Officer, Army Group Vistula, Eastern Front 1945
Hans-Georg Eismann, edited by Fred Steinhardt   ISBN 1-874622-43-4

In the Fire of the Eastern Front: The Experiences of a Dutch Waffen-SS Volunteer
on the Eastern Front 1941–45
Hendrick C. Verton   ISBN 1-874622-54-X

HELION & COMPANY

26 Willow Road, Solihull, West Midlands, B91 1UE, England
Tel 0121 705 3393   Fax 0121 711 4075
Email: publishing@helion.co.uk   Website: http://www.helion.co.uk